365 Days

OF

ARCHANGEL
MESSAGES

ANGEL GUIDANCE & JOURNAL FOR MORE PEACE, HEALING, ABUNDANCE, FINANCIAL STABILITY, AND SPIRITUAL WISDOM

KIMBERLY DAWN

365 days of Archangel messages from the following Archangels:

Archangel Michael
Archangel Raphael
Archangel Zadkiel
Archangel Uriel
Archangel Raziel
Archangel Chamuel
Archangel Gabriel
Archangel Jophiel
Archangel Ariel
Archangel Daniel
Archangel Haniel
Archangel Metatron
Archangel Jeremiel

Disclaimer

Kimberly is not a medical doctor and does not practice medicine. Kimberly doesn't diagnose, heal, cure or treat disease. Kimberly recommends people continue to see their medical doctors and follow their advice. Kimberly's work and the use of the Spiritual Cleansing (Archangels) Crystal Lights℠ is a complement to conventional medicine. You should always consult a qualified healthcare professional with questions about any medical condition. We make no claims or guarantees regarding anyone's personal experiences or results from reading this book. By continuing to read this book you agree that Kimberly and her Company are not responsible any results you experience.

My Prayer for You

I know you were led to find this book for a reason.

May you receive all the healing, love, joy, abundance, vibrancy, prosperity, connection and peace that is waiting for you through these Archangels messages.

May you know how loved you are. May you feel divine wisdom flood your veins as you read the Archangel's carefully chosen words in these passages.

May you choose to read the book starting from Day 1 – Day 365 or may the Archangels help you navigate to a page of the day to see what message it holds for you.

If you should be in sorrow, may you be healed through the Archangel healing frequencies of love and healing that will be sent to you through the Archangels words without question.

Should you need upliftment, love, comfort, soul nourishment or peace, may you hear your personal message that speaks to the heart through the words the Archangels had me type onto these pages.

With the messages that touch you profoundly, the Archangels had me type them especially for you because as you read them, you're being touched by the Archangels with healing light codes that transcend the words themselves.

Think of you reading this book as your profound and personal way of being affected by the Archangels with miracles, love, and sweetness waiting for you within each page you navigate to.

May you feel solace sent to you for any suffering you have endured in this lifetime or other lifetimes.

And may you be freed from all suffering once and for all.

In Love and Grace,

Kimberly

PS I invite you to use this book as a journal to take notes in or brainstorm any inspiring thoughts that come to you at the bottom of each Archangel message.

How Many Angels Do You See?

Below is a photo I took in Silver City, New Mexico. Some of my clients have found up to 3 Angels in this cloud photo.

How many Angels do you see?

Day 1 - Archangel Michael

"You are right on track with your expansion. You heard the call correctly. We are grinning from ear to ear for you and what is about to unfold in your life. Blessings upon blessings along with the kind of joy that makes a blue jay hop from tree to tree are here for you now. You are infinitely blessed as you continue putting one foot in front of the other with innocent anticipation. You are being made anew. Now your wings can spread and catch the harmony flight that's ahead."

Notes, inspired writing or other brainstorming ideas...

Day 2 - Archangel Raphael

"Your consciousness resides in multiple places at once. The "all" of you sees how things are possible. The part of you that is in this physical body has more capabilities than it thinks it has. You are not a meager human hoping things will work out. You are a Divine Being of Light who knows she will and is working diligently from behind the scenes creating numerous pathways for yourself at all times."

Notes, inspired writing or other brainstorming ideas...

Day 3 — Archangel Michael

"We are sending you freedom frequencies of healing. We send these to all of the earth and all of her people today for deep seeded strongholds to be transformed with ease and freedom for all to be obtained in alignment to the Divine Will for the planet. We hold up a cheer for you, to be on earth at this time is quite the ride, is it not? We salute you for your bravery. We honor you for your strength. What has been waiting eons of time to occur is happening now. Continue to be brave. Keep yourself up to receiving our strength and love. It is in the receiving of Divine Light that all will be freed. We anchor the light of strength into your heart and soul today. Breathe this in, for it is time for all of the shackles to fall away now for the entire planet and you. We love you and are with you in body, mind, and soul."

Notes, inspired writing or other brainstorming ideas . . .

Day 4 — Archangel Michael

"You have waited a long time for this moment. This is a pivotal point that picks you up higher and lifts you to the heavens so that your own heaven on earth unfolds most graciously for you. Deep breaths are needed with sighs of relief, for the easier way is here. We take your hand and walk you to a new mountain of hope, happiness, faith, and love. All is and will be more than well."

Notes, inspired writing or other brainstorming ideas...

Day 5 – Archangel Michael

"Infinite resources are available to you. The fountainhead of infinite blessings aligns for you and all around you as you step into Divine Love. When you reach too far outside of yourself thinking something you want is "out there" it places you in misalignment with Divine Intelligence. When you are just to the left of Divine Intelligence, reaching over there – you are not trusting that a Divine Wellspring of Love can be tapped from within. Opening yourself to what feels like never-ending support, love, forgiveness, and kindness places you in the continuous stream of Divine Treasures that have been waiting to reach you for eons of time."

Notes, inspired writing or other brainstorming ideas...

Day 6 – Archangel Uriel

"Let peace be in your heart today. All are being taken care of. Follow the inner promptings of when to do what. You are being guided beyond what your eyes are capable of seeing in front of you. Allow your heart to be filled with joyous visions. Many more delightful opportunities will be opening up for you. Let the openings that sing to your heart be the ones that propel you forward. Trust yourself. Be the love that you are and joyously let in all the goodness that is here for you now."

Notes, inspired writing or other brainstorming ideas...

Day 7 – Archangel Raziel

"You have so much love to give. Let the love pour through your heart like spring flowers blossoming open with the sunlight. We support you and what you are called to do. What inspires you is the true magic of the highest happenings. You are shinier than the brightest star as you follow your inner promptings of inspiration. Trust that we have your back. Continue shining brightly through your heart. As you do, your glow nourishes other hearts ready to blossom open."

Notes, inspired writing or other brainstorming ideas...

Day 8 — Archangel Michael

"Your Divine Nature wants to shine through and be the real you. We are helping the real you sing your Divine Song. In doing so, you assist the entire planet with Divine Songs of Love that brings light to those who feel separate from the light of themselves. When you hold your songs within you and don't let them out to not ruffle feathers, you prevent yourself from feeling the freedom that is yours. We encourage you to let your music out so others may dance to it. For the Divine Grace, they are most in need of is waiting for your song to be played."

Notes, inspired writing or other brainstorming ideas...

Day 9 – Archangel Michael

"Yes is the answer of the day. Yes, go for what you are being propelled forward with. The nudges we give you from the Angelic Realm become increasingly stronger as you expand beyond what you previously thought you were capable of. If you are guided to rest, rest. If you have inklings to be near water, do. Do the things that you may have held yourself back from out of feeling like you may not be enough. The zing in your step comes from your ever-growing connection to worlds of celebration beyond this world that is raising you up to be that which you already are. We are all cheering for you. The time is ripe for this. Cheers to the real you."

Notes, inspired writing or other brainstorming ideas...

Day 10 — Archangel Gabriel

"We celebrate with you new beginnings. Cheers to old and new friends coming together for a unified purpose of unfolding. What your heart would most like to have happened will be much easier to unfold this year. The energy alignment through pure heartfelt thought brings what would be for your highest and best onto center stage. Be ready to have ten times the amount of joy come into your life. The time is ripe for this, and you are ready."

Notes, inspired writing or other brainstorming ideas...

Day 11 — Archangel Jophiel

"There is so much support for you and your ideas from all of the Angelic Kingdom. We will show you which doors are most joyful for you to open and walk through. If you walk through one door and it feels like you are sinking in mud, try another door; there is always a more jovial, extended path to walk into. One must be willing to test the waters a bit and see which entry point feels more buoyant, yet grounded at the same time. Trust your internal guidance system, for this is how we send you signals of yes or no."

Notes, inspired writing or other brainstorming ideas...

Day 12 – Archangel Raphael

"Bringing more sweet times into your life heals the heart. Cherishing the tender moments brings more of them. What will bring you that delicious nurturing feeling right now? …This week? Relax in knowing I will be helping you with that. The treasure of life is in the sweetness."

Notes, inspired writing or other brainstorming ideas . . .

Day 13 – Archangel Michael

"This is a time of great change. The shifts you feel from within are genuine. Now is the time to forgive all that you feel you should have done in the past. What is most important moving forward is to focus upon your connection to your soul and the Divine. For it is in this connection with spirit that you are given the instructions of what inspired action to take next. Drinking the fresh waters of Divine *nurturance* are what so many are thirsty for at this time. The more you drink the Divine waters of love that are here for you from us and spirit, the more each step you are to take becomes crystal clear. As the old strongholds break free, your mental, emotional, physical health and stability come from aligning to your true source of power daily."

Notes, inspired writing or other brainstorming ideas...

Day 14 — Archangel Michael

"They know not what they say or do, is something significant to remember. When you do not feel understood or when others take what you said the wrong way, this is a good phrase to repeat to yourself. Right now the earth and humanity are releasing heavier frequencies that are of confusion energy. We are helping to transform these lower distortion type energies from getting in the way of the true Divine connection that is your birthright. To release chaos energy, call upon me and I will clear your thoughts and the surrounding area of confusion, thought forms and vibrations. Releasing stagnant energy will help you reach higher states of awareness with more ease and gentleness."

Notes, inspired writing or other brainstorming ideas...

Day 15 – Archangel Haniel

"Your ideas matter. Trust the inspiration coming to you. We give you new thoughts of how your life can be even more vibrant, abundant and full of joy and laughter. It is easier now than ever to realize your dreams. The old structures and thought forms are falling away. Make a beeline to your dreams because the way will continue to get easier and become more fulfilling. We love your never-ending quest of discovering more."

Notes, inspired writing or other brainstorming ideas . . .

Day 16 — Archangel Metatron

"The frequencies coming in for you for transformation are very strong right now. You are supported with elevating anything that feels like it is not quite flowing. There's a reason when hiccups happen. It presents you with an opportunity to sift, allowing the gems to come to the surface. As you extract the gems from the situation, ideas or circumstances, give yourself a night or two to process what may work better. Ask us to assist with helping you integrate the upgraded blueprints so that they feel grounded from within. You are right on track as you listen deeply to the inner signals we give you. Keep going."

Notes, inspired writing or other brainstorming ideas...

Day 17 – Archangel Michael

"All of the Archangels including myself want to assist you with clearing your chakras of any of the old pain, worry and heaviness that may reside there. The heart chakra stores so many trauma imprints in it for many on earth right now. All you have been through has not been easy, we know. Ask us to clear and transform any dread, pain, grief, resistance or heaviness for you and we will. We also bring you Divine Blessings for your heart while you sleep tonight."

Notes, inspired writing or other brainstorming ideas...

Day 18 — Archangel Michael

"Simple requests are powerful to say on your end. Whenever you make a simple request to me or the other Archangels, we are right by your side giving you love, tenderness, support and soothing energy to calm your spirit. Your prayers do not have to be complex to be heard by us. We hear your whispers for us from wherever you are. Make one simple request to me right now and you will either feel me near or receive a message or sign that miracles are being made for you in heaven."

Notes, inspired writing or other brainstorming ideas...

Day 19 – Archangel Michael

"We bring you today frequencies for seeing beyond the veil of illusion and distortion. For so many lifetimes many have not been able to receive all of their Divine Light Source. This lifetime is different. The availability to see beyond what is with great clarity is here for all. We show you what is most relevant for you to know for the next steps of your life's work. The reason why you came here is far greater than what meets the eye for many of you. It will continue to take seeing beyond the veil to know deep within what you are called to do next. All of the Archangels including myself stand next to you and support you with your soul's calling. You are already worthy. Ask, and you shall receive."

Notes, inspired writing or other brainstorming ideas...

Day 20 — Archangel Michael

"Signs from above are easy for us to bring you. All of the cosmos celebrate and dance with you when you're living your divinely inspired life daily. A shooting star that looks so breathtaking, for a moment it was mistaken for a comet in the sky. Yes, that is us gifting you with a cosmic wink. We are reminding you that you are a cosmic being in a physical body. You are infinite like we are. Your thoughts travel far beyond this world and merge with the Divine herself. Your wishes are granted and blessed by Divine Mother as your will aligns with hers. In surrendering your will to Divine Mother's will, the resources she grants you endlessly wrap the globe in blankets of love, upliftment, good health, regeneration, and healing for all."

Notes, inspired writing or other brainstorming ideas...

Day 21 — Archangel Raphael

"Be at peace in the center of your world. You are not missing a beat. You are never asked to overextend yourself past the point of it feeling good. Rest deeply tonight and know just how supported and loved you are. There is nothing sweeter than knowing you are rocked by the Divine's arms upon falling asleep. Let yourself feel this tenderly and know that you are loved infinitely."

Notes, inspired writing or other brainstorming ideas...

Day 22 — Archangel Metatron

"There is a window of opportunity presenting itself to you at this time. You have the ability to free yourself from all suffering. Allow us to take your hand and bring you into a sacred space, where no suffering exists only great love. In this space, we ask you to write down what it is you most need right now and give it to us, all of the Archangels. Allow yourself to then be refilled with light from me to help you feel more anchored in this Divine Love. Feel sacred geometric light refilling your entire being. You have entered into this precise moment in time for a reason. Suffering is only for a season. The season you are in now is never ending, ever flowing sacred protection, love, abundance, and joy."

Notes, inspired writing or other brainstorming ideas...

Day 23 – Archangel Michael

"Ask us for a new blueprint to see what your heart most desires to receive. Usually, there is a way to accomplish what you want with one-tenth the strenuous effort. Precise measurements can be made ahead of time to show you the best route for what you seek. You are enough. It is an honor to bring you what would help your life path the most right now."

Notes, inspired writing or other brainstorming ideas...

Day 24 – Archangel Raphael

"You are so dear to us. Let your light shine from within ever so brightly. If you feel rejection at certain points, it only means there are far greater friends waiting around the bend for your gracious hand. Do you know just how many friends are waiting for you around the globe? Waiting for your heart to meet theirs so they can shine brighter too?"

Notes, inspired writing or other brainstorming ideas...

Day 25 — Archangel Metatron

"You have not been forgotten. Trust your own inner processes. You are metamorphosing into who you already are more fully. If you are feeling out of sorts, simply rest. When you get sudden flashes of insights and inspiration, take action. We are helping your pathway become easier now. All is available as you allow this powerful unfoldment to occur."

Notes, inspired writing or other brainstorming ideas...

Day 26 – Archangel Michael

"Now is a pronounced time of returning to the source from which you came. As you've heard it is the time of the great awakening. It is happening in a different way than it ever has before in any universe or on any planet. Your ability to tune into what feels like Love to you and what doesn't is how we assist you in your processing of remembering. This is an original journey, never having been done before. We congratulate you for your bravery. Keep tuning into what feels like Love. If it doesn't feel like Love let it go for now and move towards the Love. Be one with the Love. We are with you, holding your hand and guiding you into what will work better for you. Bravo for your courage. Continue forth in our love that we blanket you with for support and encouragement daily. May you feel just how loved you truly are."

Notes, inspired writing or other brainstorming ideas . . .

Day 27 – Archangel Gabriel

"What uplifts one person assists the many. Touching one soul's life has the potential to raise the light quotient of millions. Grass roots movements and profound collaborations all began with one seed of an idea. The betterment of all happens in those moments when you are propelled forward to make one small bit of difference in the life of one person. The seeds of peace exist within everyone. As you continue to listen to the smallest grain of an idea you are being supported by authentic power from the Divine to bring revolutionary peace to every nation, every city, every continent and every ocean that has any kind of disturbance happening. To be alive on earth right now with the intent of peace and healing for all, you help anchor that light in for everyone. It all starts from flooding in that peace within you, today, right here, right now."

Notes, inspired writing or other brainstorming ideas...

Day 28 – Archangel Michael

"When you have resistance towards something, slow down and ask yourself, "What is it I really want that I'm not allowing myself to have?" This will clarify things for you. When you gain a clearer picture of what would help you the most, we bring in teams of assistance for you that will be working on resolutions diligently from behind the scenes. The resistance mostly comes from a need to self protect. When you request our help in this way we bring you solutions that free your soul. It is our honor to serve you in this way. Thank you for your requests, for none of them are too enormous or minute."

Notes, inspired writing or other brainstorming ideas...

Day 29 – Archangel Jeremiel

"There are easier resolutions to that which concerns you that you may not see yet. Ask us to make available the best possible outcome for all involved. New opportunities will be knocking at your door very soon. Always at your service."

Notes, inspired writing or other brainstorming ideas...

Day 30 — Archangel Zadkiel

"Sudden shifts are happening right now within so many of you. We ask you not to be afraid of any change that you are being called to make at this time. Call upon us to assist you with what steps to take and when. We will make the stepping stones more visible. At first they may feel wobbly, but as you continue taking them your life will be a memorable adventure of passionate expansion."

Notes, inspired writing or other brainstorming ideas...

Day 31 – Archangel Uriel

"Your requests are heard, do not doubt this. Write down what you want our help with daily, so we may delegate much assistance for you. Did you know we have teams of angels who are waiting to help and assist you in every way they possibly can? The more specific the better. We are with you every step of the way."

Notes, inspired writing or other brainstorming ideas...

Day 32 — Archangel Michael

"True love does come around more than once in a lifetime. True love comes in many forms. Mutual respect and honoring where the other is on their soul's path helps trust be built on fertile soil that will nourish you and the other. Even in friendships… if the give and take feels more out of a "need" than a true honoring of where the other soul is on their path, it can become draining on one or both individuals. Where there is deep listening, without it having to take any certain form in order to fill a void in one or both individuals, there is a blossoming of love that can assist both to expand beyond their current horizons."

Notes, inspired writing or other brainstorming ideas...

Day 33 – Archangel Chamuel

"Dear One, you are so beautiful inside and out. Trust yourself with knowing what is best for you. Only you know what is ultimately going to bring you happiness and joy. Go within each morning and ask what will bring you the most joy this morning and listen closely… for these are your clues to the unfolding of your soul's purpose. Be in that state of love throughout your day and you won't miss a beat."

Notes, inspired writing or other brainstorming ideas...

Day 34 – Archangel Ariel

"When you hit a brick wall or can't see past the fence, ask for my help. I help you see beyond the current horizon. You have the ability to transform any worry in your life right now with greater ease than you may be allowing yourself. Choose one area, problem or obstacle you'd like me to assist you with today and write it down. I will place my blessings upon it and all that is required from you is to be easy on yourself… for the time has come to just allow divine abundance, blessings and love to be bestowed upon you. It is my honor to assist in this way. The love you feel today is my presence of love and upliftment with you."

Notes, inspired writing or other brainstorming ideas...

Day 35 – Archangel Raziel

"Trust the transitions that are occurring. You are right on track with everything. We are here supporting you every step of the way. All is lining up for your greater good now. There are lovely new people and events entering into your arena that will bring even more blessings, love and connection. Allow your heart to continue to unfold and be joyous of new happenings."

Notes, inspired writing or other brainstorming ideas...

Day 36 – Archangel Zadkiel

"When someone is negative towards you, take it as a sign that you have moved beyond extensive limitations from within yourself. What you are being guided to do, be or have is specifically unique for your soul's calling which has nothing to do with other's doubts or fears. You didn't come here to bar yourself up, you came here to fly like a freedom dove in the bluest skies of all."

Notes, inspired writing or other brainstorming ideas...

Day 37 – Archangel Michael

"When you energize your space, environment and everyday life with empowered thoughts of higher intentions, it helps us create magnetic life formations for you. We bring in geometric light structures that sustain these good intentions for your world. It is an honor for us to bring these crystalline light structures in for you so that you may hold higher more vibrant states of being for your health and your creations. You make it easier for us to ground in strengthening light structures for the planet with your prayers, mantras, uplifting thoughts and good intentions for all. This brings hope, peace, safety and love to others in the vicinity and world at large."

Notes, inspired writing or other brainstorming ideas...

Day 38 – Archangel Michael

"Behind the scenes Divine orchestrations are taking places for everyone on earth right now who has raised their hands on the etheric planes. Some are being asked to move to specific locations on earth for the purpose of lighting up that section of earth with light we send through you. Some are being asked to remain where they are and bring in more light through prayer, sacred song and study of sacred text. Some are being asked to go to locations at different times of the year to disperse the light code frequencies we send through you – near beaches, for the wild life in the oceans. However you are being called, know you will be supported with the way being made for you. Divine flow always supports those with sincere hearts."

Notes, inspired writing or other brainstorming ideas...

Day 39 – Archangel Ariel

"When you feel like you want to be in charge of your life completely, we invite you to ask Divine Mother to show you the way. Divine Mother sees for you which direction would bring you the absolute peace, joy, love and connection your heart is longing for. Surrender your will to hers and she will take care of you for the rest of your days here upon the earth. She is the great mender and healer. She sees a better way for you than you can see for yourself. Allow her to take your hand and show you where the rose petals are. Following her blessed rose petals she places before your feet will lead you to the most comforting soul rich earth experience you can imagine. She holds out her hand for you now and says, 'Come over here, look at these joy love blossoms I have placed for you just ahead…'"

Notes, inspired writing or other brainstorming ideas…

Day 40 — Archangel Metatron

"You think you are alone in so much that you do, but you are not. You always have a ladder to the higher realms… to us. We are right next to you, showing you new options daily. Hitting a wall just means keep knocking and asking… soon an exhilarating door will appear and open. You are so beautiful, if you could only see yourself through our eyes. You would realize just how much you are being guided every moment in your earth journey. Take breaks as needed, but keep asking… exuberant possibilities you never knew existed will be presenting themselves."

Notes, inspired writing or other brainstorming ideas . . .

Day 41 – Archangel Raphael

"Sometimes when people throw a fit it is but a cry for love. That is all they know to do when the isolation feeling is so great within them. As you connect in deeply with Source, The Divine and heal your own feelings of separation, this gives the other person the ability to do the same. Similar to the 100th monkey effect. Tantrum throwers want to know they are not alone, most of all. You connecting to the peace within shows them they can attain that connection too. It all starts with you. No amount of "fixing" or rearranging circumstances can compare to the resolutions that will come from syncing up to your own peace stream."

Notes, inspired writing or other brainstorming ideas...

Day 42 — Archangel Michael

"You facing your fears head on helps us integrate those aspects of yourself that have been hurt in the past (even past lives) into wholeness again. Some run in circles their entire lives as they avoid facing their deepest fears. Those parts of yourself may be trying to protect others parts of self; this is very normal. Asking any of the Archangels (including myself) to help you face your fears and integrate parts of yourself that may be scared and disconnected from the larger part of you (who always knows you are taken care of) brings clarity, peace and connection to you and the world at large. As you allow all parts of self to integrate into wholeness again others can do this too through your example of self love."

Notes, inspired writing or other brainstorming ideas...

Day 43 – Archangel Raphael

"The love we have for you and all of humanity is unyielding, never ending and always available for you. We are so pleased to bring you higher frequencies of peace, serenity, support and upliftment. When you call my name I am there in less than a second, standing with you. You have not been forgotten. What once used to take years to transform into a higher way of being or doing things can now be done in a very short amount of time because the veil is getting thinner and you can more readily receive the healing frequencies we are sending you. You are part of us, so to assist you is raising the light quotient for all."

Notes, inspired writing or other brainstorming ideas...

Day 44 – Archangel Michael

"Go with the brightest star within your heart, for this will ignite the passageway for others. Inside your heart is the star from which you came. It is time to let this starlight out to play and blaze the freedom trail you're here to deliver. We support your ideas no matter how outlandish they may seem to others around you. For what we show you in your heart of hearts is your immortal star that cannot be dimmed by other's opinions of you or circumstances that seem impossible to overcome. Allowing yourself to shine brightly is the real you."

Notes, inspired writing or other brainstorming ideas...

Day 45 – Archangel Michael

"Close your eyes (if you'd like) and feel, sense or see what is pulling on your energy. What is draining your energy right now? Whatever is causing you to feel tired, place this into a golden ball of light and hand the golden ball of energy to me with your energy drains within it. Ask me to transform these areas for you and bring you more viable solutions. All of the Archangels will be working on this for you overnight. Be prepared to receive more resolutions in the days to come…for it is our honor to do this for you."

Notes, inspired writing or other brainstorming ideas…

Day 46 – Archangel Raphael

"You are trusting your innermost promptings more and more and we are so pleased. More abundance in all areas of your life are ready to flood in now. What brings you harmony magnetizes your desires. What brings you discord pushes it further away. The loveliness of your expanded awareness into more blissful acceptance of what you truly want has created a sphere of love vibrations that create your time and space reality to be moments of inhaled goodness with only more sweetness to come. We honor your ability to tune in and listen so intently because it is in that connection we are able to bring even more of your most cherished desires to you in delightful ways."

Notes, inspired writing or other brainstorming ideas...

Day 47 – Archangel Gabriel

"Love heals all wounds. This cliché is absolutely the truth of it. You have the capacity to heal from all of the hurts, pains, abandonment, regret and any angst through the purifying, healing salve of Divine Love and Grace. Immersing yourself in a state of peace and love instead of letting the fears create endless wheels of needless spinning images in your head, heightens your realization that you ARE LOVE. You came here to Love. You are Love. You are loved infinitely and forever. Ask yourself how you can give love to someone or something today from a place of total peace, love and connection in your heart. As you give love from this state of being, you are quadrupling the love that boomerangs back to you in unexpected multitudes of diverse ways."

Notes, inspired writing or other brainstorming ideas...

Day 48 — Archangel Michael

"We are so pleased to see you when you are smiling. What feels like a long journey is now being accomplished in a very short amount of time. More joy is ready to spring forth in your life in numerous ways. It has been so delightful to see your expansion process. It is an honor to walk with you on your journey."

Notes, inspired writing or other brainstorming ideas...

Day 49 – Archangel Michael

"There are so many rewards coming to you as you continue to honor your true feelings. Spontaneous wishes are fulfilled. All you have desired will continue coming to fruition as you honor your true nature."

Notes, inspired writing or other brainstorming ideas...

Day 50 – Archangel Michael

"You are being guided and led to higher grounds every step of the way. What helps you create the most beautiful creations of all is the joy of each step you are being led to take. Not getting too far ahead of yourself with anything, but fully indulging in moment by moment listening. Here you will feel the most stable and connected. There is nothing that is too far out of reach that doesn't begin with the first delightful step. What raises you up with a smile gives others a reason to smile too."

Notes, inspired writing or other brainstorming ideas...

Day 51 – Archangel Raphael

"This is the time to allow the old triggers to come to the surface. Guilt and shame are outworn frequencies on earth that have held mankind down for a very long time. Now is the hour to break free of confinements of the heart and soul. Call upon me to uproot the core issues completely. Your heart deserves to be as free as a songbird. Ask me to lift the scary parts that sometimes holds you back and what you'll find is your pot of gold, your heaven on earth, at the end of your rainbow that wraps the earth in your soul-shine-brilliance."

Notes, inspired writing or other brainstorming ideas...

Day 52 – Archangel Michael

"What you see, sense and feel is very real. Too often we watch the most gifted souls dismiss what they are sensing. What you are sensing is us trying to tell you the direction that would be best for you. Heed these innermost promptings, for they are valid and we are guiding you to the most exquisite freedom-lands through your inner navigation system. You are worthy of the truth and the truth shall set you free."

Notes, inspired writing or other brainstorming ideas...

Day 53 – Archangel Ariel

"Your alignment begins to happen when you let go, focusing on what truly matters to your heart and soul. Your intentions are very powerful when aligned to what would assist the good of all. You have what it takes. Keep your focus with peace and grace and what you wish will easily come into fruition. Listen from within to what feels most joyful for you. Ask us to bless your projects and anything else you'd like assistance with. You are a beautiful being of light inside and out. We love you."

Notes, inspired writing or other brainstorming ideas...

Day 54 – Archangel Daniel

"Celebrate the journey all the way home. Fill your days with enjoyment segments. The bliss you generate by treating yourself as you would adore your beloved brings peace to all beings on earth. When you awaken each morning visualize one Divine treat you can give yourself that day. This will pave the way for unexpected delightful happenings to enter your experience with ease."

Notes, inspired writing or other brainstorming ideas...

Day 55 – Archangel Michael

"Sometimes what's easy sets your heart free the most. Simplifying your life helps your soul and the Archangels to rejuvenate your body systems. Ask yourself, "Where can I simplify my life so that I feel more taken care of?" What takes the pressure off brings rainbows, sunshine and flowers."

Notes, inspired writing or other brainstorming ideas...

Day 56 – Archangel Michael

"Resistance with what would bring you improved health, joy, love, prosperity and freedom is usually a sign there are parts of self that are seeking integration into wholeness again. All of the Archangels and myself know how to help these parts of yourself that have been split off receive soul level healing and integrate into wholeness again. Often times this reduces anxiety and helps you trust yourself more because the wisdom that then comes into your conscious awareness is from the Divine Wisdom that knows a higher orchestration of how your life will work better for you. The fragmented parts of self or the wounded inner child aspects that have been separated from self are often just afraid. Asking us to integrate these fragmented afraid aspects into wholeness again brings sustained and long lasting wisdom, safety, joy, love and comfort."

Notes, inspired writing or other brainstorming ideas...

Day 51 – Archangel Raphael

"Be at peace within the deepest core of yourself. You have the incredible ability to heal yourself through peaceful thoughts, prayers, intentions and connections. When you are at peace you create a healing ripple effect that reaches into the cosmos. When something is disturbing you, call upon me to help you find your tranquil center from the core of your being again. Let yourself be submerged in this blissful state as often as possible. You are honored for your dedication and service to yourself and humanity, for it is through you feeling good from the inside that your outer world is elevated and transformed."

Notes, inspired writing or other brainstorming ideas...

Day 58 — Archangel Raphael

"When one door closes abruptly we reassure you there's another door you are about to open that ushers in the most brilliant light that feels like the most soul refreshing waterfall you've ever had the pleasure of experiencing. This waterfall not only connects you, it brings you the soul food you have been seeking. Sometimes opening up new doors is nerve-wracking because you don't know what energy will greet you. Trust that the right doors for you are the ones that feel like a safe place to spread your wings and fly. Opening these doors will lift you higher right away. Your energy will not drop, it will rise. When your light meets another's light who feels like a breath of fresh air, you can be assured we are there lifting you both higher."

Notes, inspired writing or other brainstorming ideas . . .

Day 59 – Archangel Raziel

"Having a sanctuary space that is just your own helps you to bring more of your soul's gifts through. Your safe, sacred space is important for you to claim. Call us into your sacred space to bless every corner of it and raise its frequency several octaves higher. If everyone on earth did this there would be far fewer wars on earth. What is anchored in on one continent is felt on its polar opposite instantly, no exception. You have the power to bring peace to many nations through the sacred safe space you create to connect to the peace that is always available for you. Archangel Michael stands guard around you (as you ask him to) so you may be at peace, anytime, anyplace."

Notes, inspired writing or other brainstorming ideas...

Day 60 — Archangel Gabriel

"You are an incredibly gifted soul. We bring you today a gift, in a white box with your favorite colored bow. Open now and see what the box has in it for you. There is a message for you with this gift, see what it wants you to know right now…Ahhhh… there is plenty of time for all that your heart longs for. Rest assured, all that you want is coming."

Notes, inspired writing or other brainstorming ideas...

Day 61 – Archangel Michael

"When your energy system, auric field and energy bodies have been cleared of lower interferences and blockages in the energy channels, you receive new blueprints for easier more efficient ways of doing things more readily because your energy bodies are connected up to a higher support system that sustains the new forms easier. What causes difficulties for individuals is when they hang onto "old form" ways of doing things when what their high self is really ready for is a newer, more sustainable way of being. Syncing up with high self in this way helps us bring you higher blueprints (that your soul is ready for you to have) which will make it much easier for you to bring your dreams into form here in the physical. Ask us to assist you in this way and so shall it be. It is our honor."

Notes, inspired writing or other brainstorming ideas...

Day 62 – Archangel Metatron

"Time is changing as you know it on earth. You can go into "no time" to receive years of instruction, encapsulated into an hour of your earth time. This is why meditation is so vital right now with all the earth changes. Call upon me to assist you with receiving upgraded blueprints of instruction for your next steps that are aligned to the higher consciousness plan for humanity. These will help you bypass the old ways of doing things and bring you easier solutions for everything in your life. These blueprints will not only help raise consciousness for all of humanity, they assist you in finding alternate solutions that feel more joyful."

Notes, inspired writing or other brainstorming ideas...

Day 63 — Archangel Michael

"The things that cause you to feel stressed out can be a blessing in disguise. Asking yourself the questions, "What would I prefer instead of this stress?" and "How may I begin to create this in my world?" Answering both of these questions allows us to bring you new ideas of how you can transform stressful things into more peace, joy, love and abundance. As the old form ways of doing things transcend into the new blueprints for your life, peace arrives at your front door more and more."

Notes, inspired writing or other brainstorming ideas...

Day 64 – Archangel Michael

"We hand you a bouquet of your favorite colored roses today. We take the thorns out for you. Smelling the rose buds of your life and watching in awe as they blossom, brings you the sweet essence of creation itself day after day, year after year. You have entered into a new season today. You are growing younger by the day because the youth of you that delights in the ever expanding creation process never grows old. The delights, the joy-treasures, the river of creative supply is never ending – so too are you never ending, always beginning, spreading your wings and taking flight into the possibilities that are already you."

Notes, inspired writing or other brainstorming ideas...

Day 65 – Archangel Haniel

"Simplifying things makes your life so much more expansive and fun. All you want is in the simplification. The pure essence of love, peace and good feeling thoughts creates momentum faster than anything. What does it "feel" like to have the essence of what you want? Feel this today and we will be assisting with many blessings easily falling into your lap."

Notes, inspired writing or other brainstorming ideas . . .

Day 66 – Archangel Michael

"Sometimes what is simple, easy and effortless for you is the solution you have been seeking. What feels like breathing to you may not be what others are best at. Effortless creation of your dreams without over thinking them into complexity helps you know which direction we are pointing you towards. What gets your stomach in knots usually means there are repercussions with something you have been pondering. When you are in the flow of your Divine inspiration, there may be a small incline up the hill but it will feel clear, simple, grounded and steady."

Notes, inspired writing or other brainstorming ideas...

Day 67 — Archangel Raphael

"There is celebration beyond belief for you realizing just how loved you are. Making waves is a connecting act of loving kindness. When you make waves with what your soul is calling you to do each and every day you create a ripple effect that helps everyone around you make the changes they need to make more easily as well."

Notes, inspired writing or other brainstorming ideas...

Day 69 – Archangel Raziel

"Keep focusing on what you would prefer. You are doing such a wonderful job our friend. You have the ability to create what your heart is telling you would be better for you. You are a very unique soul here on earth. Trust the process of unfoldment and have fun with it like sliding down the most exhilarating slide ever ridden. We are with you having just as much fun watching you and supporting you every step of the way. You are beautiful inside and out. We love you."

Notes, inspired writing or other brainstorming ideas...

Day 70 — Archangel Michael

"Your heart is in the right place as you ask to be shown what is for the highest and best good of all. You cannot make the wrong move by asking this each day. It can be simpler than you are expecting. We assure you, so much goodness, love, comfort and grace will fill your life naturally from doing so."

Notes, inspired writing or other brainstorming ideas...

Day 71 – Archangel Zadkiel

"Your inner wisdom knows how worthy you are. You are ready for more. Make the request and so shall it be. There is enough time in the day to create and receive what your heart's desire is. We bring you greater wisdom today of "how" to allow this in through grace."

Notes, inspired writing or other brainstorming ideas...

Day 72 – Archangel Zadkiel

"Do what's for your highest and best good. You'll know with your body signals if something will create an imbalance in your system. Forgive yourself first and foremost for not being "deemed" normal. Your normal is what creates that beautiful Divine Connection that you have. You were born that way for a reason. Call upon me to release any self judgments. Life is about to get really, really good. All of us Angels are cheering you on… all the way home."

Notes, inspired writing or other brainstorming ideas...

Day 73 – Archangel Michael

"Fear not. The basis of what all humans want is love. To give love does not have to mean compromising yourself in any way shape or form. Love comes with setting healthy boundaries for self and others. When you are confused about what you want, ask yourself "What would love look like to me today?" The feelings of love can take many delightful forms. Ask us to bring you the "feeling" of what you most want and allow this feeling to dance within you, bringing you treasures from a world far more vast in richness than here. You came into this world of half dimmed darkness to ignite it with graceful wildfires of Divine Treasures lit through your heart and your imagination. As above, so below. You are worthy, this we know."

Notes, inspired writing or other brainstorming ideas...

Day 74 – Archangel Daniel

"We are assisting you with your ideas, to help you give life to them. Please do not discount any thoughts you receive that inspire and light you up. Everyone of them could grow roots and assist the earth and her inhabitants with more nourishment and upliftment that is so needed. The soil is fertile. You focusing on which seeds you want to grow will help us to energize them for you. Water them daily with joy, love, laughter and celebration. These roots are giving sustenance to Mother Earth in a multitude of ways."

Notes, inspired writing or other brainstorming ideas...

Day 75 – Archangel Raphael

"Simplifying what really matters in your life brings deep peace, healing, love and vitality to all of your cells. Your heart expands to new horizons as you simplify what means the most to you and why it does. What brings you joy uplifts all of humanity. Your joy is what helps set your heart free. We bring you blessings today of the simple sweetness that exists all around you and inside of you. Relish the sweet joys that are here now and all else will fall into place. We love you to the end of time and beyond."

Notes, inspired writing or other brainstorming ideas...

Day 76 — Archangel Ariel

"Laughter reboots the brain, energizing all the feel-good chemicals in the body. We send you frequencies of laughter sometimes to assist you with not taking any of this earth school too seriously. We love to see a smile on your face and laughter in your heart. What could you do for yourself today to help you know that, ALL is truly well? Relax into this knowingness today and feel the never ending love from us pave a smoother road ahead."

Notes, inspired writing or other brainstorming ideas...

Day 77 – Archangel Ariel

"Let your heart be free. You are riding a wave right now that will open up doors for you beyond your wildest expectations. You may get a little wind surfed but the beach on the horizon is the best one so far. Enjoy your ride into the surf, as this one has been a long time coming. The sand is the finest ever."

Notes, inspired writing or other brainstorming ideas...

Day 78 — Archangel Raphael

"You are expanding past the previous limitations you had placed upon yourself. As you continue to blossom, you'll sometimes feel an uprooting of the old happening. This means you are growing by leaps and bounds. Give yourself the time needed to get grounded, write, comfort yourself and soak up Mother Nature even more than usual so we can continue to stabilize you with deep roots. We are bringing in new light, patterns and blueprints to replace what no longer serves you or your Divine Calling. As we assist you with rewiring the new patterns, give yourself the time needed for deep integration to occur. You'll then be able to take inspired action when you feel the pull towards soul-nurturing adventures."

Notes, inspired writing or other brainstorming ideas...

Day 79 – Archangel Michael

"Things can change in a flash. We are working with you on the inner planes to assist you with all the alterations you are requesting in order to make your physical world a playground of more joy, love, harmony, peace, connection and celebration. For what you request while you sleep does have an impact on your waking hours. You are working with us to put into place many alignments along your walkway that peacefully bring you the most delightful spontaneous occurrences which elevate your consciousness and the harmony-thoughts of all whom you come into contact with."

Notes, inspired writing or other brainstorming ideas...

Day 80 – Archangel Michael

"Asking any of the Archangels how you may relieve undue pressure for yourself will bring you answers that set your spirit free. Close your eyes and ask me this question then feel into, write or sense the answers that come to you. Beautiful fresh hues in the landscape of your life are entering the horizon and are here to set your heart completely free."

Notes, inspired writing or other brainstorming ideas...

Day 81 – Archangel Jophiel

"The thread of your light is so important in the intricate weaving of light pillars on the planet. We are helping you shine your light even brighter at this time. Your brilliant light blazes a trail for numerous others on the path, so they can start shining. Without yours, hundreds of others may not flip the switch on their light pillars. Your soul makes a difference when it decides."

Notes, inspired writing or other brainstorming ideas...

Day 82 — Archangel Metatron

"Right now the frequencies of light you are able to hold are increasing greatly. The old thought forms, beliefs and resistances are coming up to the surface to be released, more now than ever. Do not beat yourself up as this is happening. You are ready and we are assisting you abundantly with this process of anchoring this new light on the planet."

Notes, inspired writing or other brainstorming ideas...

Day 83 — Archangel Ariel

"Trust that your truth is right on track for you. Let your life be a living testament to the thanksgiving and appreciation of your true self. For it is in honoring who you truly are first and foremost that you are set free and you'll be honored in return."

Notes, inspired writing or other brainstorming ideas...

Day 84 – Archangel Michael

"The light we are sending to earth right now is increasing in order to elevate those who are releasing the outworn ways of doing things from their systems and energy bodies. Struggle is no longer needed however, to move into the higher states of being we hold out our hands and bathe you in a new light. This light is here to anchor you securely into the higher dimensions of Divine Light on earth so you are a carrier of much needed light codes for the planet, so that humanity can release their suffering more easily. It's like the shedding of old skin, yes – and it is a greeting of the new self simultaneously. No longer do you have to try and do this on your own. Allow me and all the Archangels to carry you through this section of time. For it is in surrendering and letting go that your connection to heaven on earth can be embodied by you. You are not just a mere mortal, you are a Light Being here to reclaim all parts of self and integrate them (with our assistance) back into the brilliance from which you came."

Notes, inspired writing or other brainstorming ideas...

Day 85 – Archangel Michael

"When change arrives, know there's a smoother ride ahead. We are orchestrating for you positive, uplifting and life enhancing people, places and events in the coming months. What hasn't worked for you in such a long time is now going to have an effortless flow. Your willingness to surrender to the Divine plan for your life allowed us to move mountains for you. We are smiling with you today placing a circle of roses around your feet. For what comes next is better than good... it is Divine."

Notes, inspired writing or other brainstorming ideas...

Day 86 – Archangel Michael

"We are entering a time where we are able to bring you more blessings. You can feel and sense us there assisting you in a number of ways now. It is a great delight for us to bring you more support, love, upliftment and nourishment. Let your heart be free of any worries. Us assisting you with all that you have requested helps us bring great blessings to many. You are worthy of receiving this, our Dear One. More treasures and blessings to come."

Notes, inspired writing or other brainstorming ideas...

Day 87 — Archangel Michael

"Soothing tones are being played by the music Angels today. This is a time of greater understanding and awareness for you. We are bringing frequencies through to make a passageway for your will to become all the way aligned to the Divine Will. In asking us to align your will to Divine Will, the struggle transforms into alchemy of the highest accord. Your will blended with Divine Will has a far wider reach than using only your human strength. Before going to sleep tonight, you may ask your will to be blended with Divine Will and all of The Archangels and I will make this so. It is our honor to do so."

Notes, inspired writing or other brainstorming ideas...

Day 88 – Archangel Raphael

"Where are you feeling a lack of support in your life? What sadness inside do you have that needs healing? Name the longing and the sadness and I, along with the other Archangels will bring you the comfort, healing, connection and love you are craving. Going to the core like this helps us raise you higher in a moment's notice. Making the impossible real is our specialty. Nothing needs to be suppressed any longer. Write down in your notebook what it is you wish you didn't feel. Become one with this feeling now and feel our wings of love wrapped around you, anointing you with healing balms of tenderness. For your soul deserves this and you deserve to be connected to your Divine Self completely."

Notes, inspired writing or other brainstorming ideas...

Day 89 — Archangel Gabriel

"Often times the more simple the better. The pleasant route with lots of blossoming flowers is usually the humble and connected way of doing things. When you ask us, all of the Archangels, for a shorter more simplified way for you, we will always bring you a sweeter, more flowing option for any issue at hand. You do not need to spend hours figuring things out any longer. Usually a new way of doing things will just pop into your thoughts from us. Ask us for a better way, then rest, play, dance and be in love with your life. You'll soon be given the most profound idea(s) yet."

Notes, inspired writing or other brainstorming ideas...

Day 90 – Archangel Michael

"When in doubt, love it out. Mother Nature when burned does not reject herself and just stay partially dead. She brings greenery to the tiny shrubs above her surface and begins to wrap herself in healing balms of fresh rich growth of wildflowers dancing in the sunlight. She forgives and grows new limbs almost immediately. So too with you, we want you to forgive what has happened in your past and remember the sweet rejuvenating lessons of Mother Earth. Forgive, grow some more and reach towards the warm sunlight upon your face. You deserve this and so shall be the renewal of your body, mind and soul."

Notes, inspired writing or other brainstorming ideas...

Day 91 – Archangel Michael

"Restoring order to things happens when you step out of the chaos. Seeds of opportunity are presented in every chaotic situation. If the old structures are wanting to melt down, you can be sure we are there depositing seeds of fresh creative opportunity for you. Allow the chaos to occur, for this cannot be controlled. Going within to find and unfold the Divine Seeds, the light coded blueprints are where your happiest expansion blossoms into full spring, creating gardens of abundance and love for all."

Notes, inspired writing or other brainstorming ideas...

Day 92 – Archangel Metatron

"We bring you even more support teams of assistance today. Recharging your batteries when needed and asking for support from us helps us assist you at more levels. Now is a time to allow distractions to take a back seat and ask yourself what is it your heart is craving? Is it more love, support, nurturing or upliftment? Putting this into words and writing it down helps us send you these frequencies from the Divine. Trying to get these frequencies from other distraction sources only leads you further away from what the core of you is really seeking. Letting go of old habits that no longer feel good to your body, mind and soul helps us instantly send you precise Divine Source Light that brings comfort to all parts of yourself."

Notes, inspired writing or other brainstorming ideas...

Day 93 — Archangel Metatron

"As you are in this time of enlightenment on your earth school it is our honor to assist you in all ways we possibly can. When you call upon me I am here with you, right by your side, in less than the length it takes to call my name. Your cries for help are heard. This is the time of the great brightening of eyes. Your eyes are sparkling with Divine Light as the shackles fall away. What you are worthy of is a complete return back to wholeness, a return to the Source of you. There have been many pitfalls in your pathway, yes? This was not so much predestined as it was the challenges you knew you would encounter when you entered into this earth school this time around. The seemingly never-ending struggles you once encountered were not something we took lightly when we helped you prepare for reentry into this world. You knew there would be unforeseen events and energies that would try to hold you in the familiar strongholds that humans must learn how to transform. You knew you would enter into this time of massive transformation in order to help free others through your own example of becoming free. We anoint you today with more strength. For we know sometimes it takes unyielding determination on your part. The good news is, you have overcome many threshold points. In stepping beyond these junctures the deep transformation has happened completely, for those mountains have been climbed. I hold out my hand for you and send in through your crown chakra golden sacred geometry light, the light of strength for humans I have been granted by the Divine to bring you. Through this light let it be known that you will make it past all the rest of the juncture points along your path. You have the help of 1000 Saints and all of the Archangels carrying you home."

Day 94 — Archangel Michael

"Planetary shifts are happening rapidly. Many of you are being called to make swift changes in order to be in sync with your Divine flow more profoundly. As you take the steps necessary, allow yourself time to unwind and breathe in each moment fully. There is nothing to "get to", only being here in this Divine unfolding instant to simply enjoy it. We bring you frequencies of peace, love, gratitude, connection and harmony today. You have not gone too far. This juncture contains everything you need. We love you."

Notes, inspired writing or other brainstorming ideas...

Day 95 – Archangel Zadkiel

"Be kind when you rewind. There is so much happening at this time on earth that it is not possible to get everything right all the time. Doing what's best for yourself now is most important. You gain strength the moment you ask for clarity from any of the Archangels, including me. We beam light to you from the Divine Creator who supports you by allowing choices that empower you all the way. Your asking for our support allows you to be connected into Divine Knowing from a team of Angelic advisers who will help you feel from deep within what is absolutely for your highest and best good. Trust the process of asking us for more assistance, for we will be there even before you can say our name to bring you the wisdom, love and comfort you seek."

Notes, inspired writing or other brainstorming ideas...

Day 96 – Archangel Michael

"The seeds of all your heart dreams are here for you now. What you have desired for so long is ripe like the fruit on a summer plum tree. Allow yourself to be a pioneer with transforming discoveries that raise humanity's light quotient to heaven's heights. Streamline what works for you and give what no longer feels good to you, to us energetically, so we may assist you with this. For the ultimate earth quantum leap is at hand and you are playing your part within that."

Notes, inspired writing or other brainstorming ideas...

Day 97 – Archangel Raphael

"The most wonderful allowing you are doing is surrendering to the flow of where the current is taking you. We support your inspirations 100% and then some. Your ideas matter. We bring you a very sweet surprise soon as you continue unfolding what makes your life the sweetest and brings it the most joy. You never need to expend so much effort that it throws you off balance. Your giving starts with yourself first. Trust this. You are loved infinitely and forever."

Notes, inspired writing or other brainstorming ideas...

Day 98 – Archangel Michael

"Allow your energy system to be purified today with envisioning and feeling yourself bathed under an island waterfall of nurturing love and unified acceptance. Divine Mother anoints you through this waterfall frequency so all that has been troubling you is washed away. Picture the abundance, love and harmony you seek while under Divine Mother's aqua fresh. For what she gifts you with here is made so, with ease and grace this day forevermore."

Notes, inspired writing or other brainstorming ideas...

Day 99 – Archangel Michael

"You are being reinvigorated today with a new freedom blueprint. If you say yes to receiving an upgraded emotional, mental, spiritual and physical freedom template, be ready for miraculous new beginnings to present themselves. Whenever you feel you are dragging yourself through mud or your thoughts feel heavy, please do ask us for upgraded angelic blueprints. This way what will set you free on all levels becomes easily available to you in the form of ideas, your gifts enhanced, aha-moments and doors opening unexpectedly. All of the Angelic Kingdom has ladders available for you and humanity at this time. You are worth receiving a lift off into bluer skies and the sweet joy songs of hummingbird days. Ask and ye shall receive and it is so."

Notes, inspired writing or other brainstorming ideas...

Day 100 – Archangel Gabriel

"You are on the brink of discovering something incredibly special. Write your inspired ideas down because they will continue to open up and reveal themselves to you with evergreen inspiration. You are already forgiven for any misperception of truth you have about what you "should" or "shouldn't" be doing. Your joy is the sign post that hosts rainbow clouds of new beginnings for you. The lands of enchantment you are embarking upon will spring forth exuberant wild flowers all around the earth that will bring light coded seeds to those who didn't even know they were looking for them."

Notes, inspired writing or other brainstorming ideas...

Day 101 – Archangel Raguel

"Trust that you are being guided. What you most want IS possible. There are so many friends, resources and people being sent to you that you cannot see yet. Have faith that all is working out in alignment to your soul's greater good. Keep on tuning in deeply to source energy and let go of what no longer serves you or your life purpose. Spring time is coming and you are breaking new ground with it."

Notes, inspired writing or other brainstorming ideas...

Day 102 – Archangel Daniel

"For centuries we couldn't reach the people as easily as we can now. This time on earth is like no other. So many can hear, feel, sense and see us now. We literally take your prayers and intentions and deliver them to your delegating team so you have more support and help immediately! Things do not have to take a millennium anymore. Ask us today for what you most want and need, place this on the silver platter I hold for you, and watch miraculous events occur this next week. Yours truly, in service to you always."

Notes, inspired writing or other brainstorming ideas...

Day 103 – Archangel Michael

"There's so much goodness ready to burst forth in your life. The love of you knows this. Allow yourself to receive Divine Love today from us. Rest in the goodness of yourself today, instead of looking at fixing or improving anything. The goodness of you is connected to the most sustaining love you'll ever find. Bathe in the love that is you."

Notes, inspired writing or other brainstorming ideas...

Day 104 — Archangel Raguel

"You are supported beyond what your mind can comprehend. The Divine has you in the palm of his/her hands. Feel a flood of liquid golden love enter your entire being from the Divine today. By bathing in this golden light of support you are receiving the Divine's Will as already done. This activates your soul's gifts to blossom forth in total and complete fulfillment aligned with the highest and best good of all. The light of who you are knows your worthiness. Be one with this wellspring of continuous light and know that any worries and troubles of the mind are like a tiny bit of dust that holds no power over you or your soul's calling."

Notes, inspired writing or other brainstorming ideas...

Day 105 – Archangel Daniel

"You are celebrated beyond belief today. This lifetime has proven challenging, yes? There is no better time than beginning right where you are. Your cosmic light is meant to touch thousands of lives and already is. The higher part of you assists many while you are sleeping. You are ready and the time is now."

Notes, inspired writing or other brainstorming ideas . . .

Day 106 – Archangel Daniel

"Let go. Claim joy. Bring peace. You are celebrated today for your courage. What no longer brings you joy has been replaced with unlimited flowers at your doorstep ready to be transplanted into your garden of peace. Plant the flowers that most feel like love to your soul. You bring possibility to all of humanity when you choose the flowers that usher in peace and elation. What springs forth are fresh creative flowers multiplying daily for others to plant in their gardens of possibility."

Notes, inspired writing or other brainstorming ideas...

Day 107 – Archangel Ariel

"Be kind to yourself in your mind. Be your own best friend of encouragement. All of us are working FOR you all the time, not against you. When you ride the wave of negative internal dialogue you place yourself against yourself and you cannot hear our loving thoughts, upliftment and inspiration for you. How can you give yourself the utmost love and respect today? Go there inside. Be one with that energy."

Notes, inspired writing or other brainstorming ideas...

Day 108 – Archangel Michael

"Call upon me when you feel out of sorts or need any lower vibrations or frequencies raised higher. I will transform whatever has been dragging you down. With my sword, all cords that need to be cut and released from pulling or draining your energy system will be released and taken to a better place and transformed into more light from the Divine. We are at a junction point on earth right now when you can ask Divine Will to make it happen and it will be made so. The blocks and interferences are being removed. You do not have to suffer any longer. This is important for you to know. All of the old ways of doing things are brought to a higher state of continuous peace from within. Ask for peace, abundance, joy and complete inner freedom and it shall be so."

Notes, inspired writing or other brainstorming ideas...

Day 109 – Archangel Azriel

"Sometimes deep rest is needed after many action steps. Balancing rest and play create happy rhythms in the body. There is so much light, energy and support here for you from us. Rest assured all you want is coming and already exists. It can be no other way. You are cherished and loved through eternity and back by us."

Notes, inspired writing or other brainstorming ideas...

Day 110 — Archangel Ariel

"Dimming your light for others does not help the collective whole of humanity shine their light brighter. One light dimming for another person lowers the collective light. Sparkle your light with Divine Love and you ignite a torch that holds within it the power to ignite a million other souls on earth brighter. Yes, you may look different and be "out of the norm" in doing so, but that which is seeking to lift you higher cannot reach you if you are dimming down your light for the sake of not wanting to make someone else uncomfortable. Perhaps that person needs to feel uncomfortable to finally make the changes their soul has been trying to get them to make. When shining your light brightly, backlash only adds more light to the equation. Amplify what matters most to your heart and soul. Become the more of you all the way, without hiding in anyone else's shadow. We strengthen your light today, for this is why you came here… to be the grace that you really are."

Notes, inspired writing or other brainstorming ideas...

Day 111 – Archangel Ariel

"Your love of where you are matters most. You have so much to give. We are supporting you with your true heart's desires. You are an incredibly gifted soul. We are helping you line up to who you truly are even more succinctly. Picture and feel what you most want right now in your mind and heart and allow us to flood it with light as you breathe. What you want is easier than you think. Be there now. You are enough. The way is being paved and mountains are moving."

Notes, inspired writing or other brainstorming ideas...

Day 112 — Archangel Uriel

"Feel the sweet love here for you today. We bring you leis and a thousand flower petals for the joy you are bringing humanity just by being you. Great love is here to stay for you. Let your soul's light shine up to heaven's breath within the heartbeat of the Divine. Let the brightness of who you are be felt with the acknowledgment that all you want is for a purpose… a reason. This is the season to allow your vast cosmic light to wrap the entire globe."

Notes, inspired writing or other brainstorming ideas . . .

Day 113 – Archangel Jeremiel

"You have captivating energy. As you are true to yourself in every way possible, others take notice and can align to their truth more easily. You did not come here to people please or to bend over backwards for other people's wishes for you when it is not in alignment to what your soul is showing you is best for you. Others may not always agree with you and that's okay. You agreeing with you brings deep soul serenity. Abundance, blessings and joy are drawn to you through your alignment with source. We congratulate you for holding true to you."

Notes, inspired writing or other brainstorming ideas...

Day 114 – Archangel Raphael

"Celebration abounds for your courage in showing up each day and listening to the promptings from within. You braved many storms. The richness of life is here for you to enjoy fully now. You have been carried across the threshold and will continue to be. We bring you your favorite flowers today… your life will continue to unfold in magical ways."

Notes, inspired writing or other brainstorming ideas...

Day 115 — Archangel Ariel

"In this moment, we send you frequencies of "All Is Well". Nothing to do. Nowhere to be. This moment brings with it everything you desire and more. You are enough. You have enough. Your life is enough right here, right now. Congratulations. You have arrived. Take a deep breath, for what you most want already is."

Notes, inspired writing or other brainstorming ideas...

Day 116 – Archangel Michael

"Forgive them, for they know not what they do. When you are triggered by someone else's verbiage, reactions or lack thereof we remind you today that this old pain that may feel as fresh as a bleeding wound sometimes is ready to be unhooked from your system all the way. Remember when you feel poked, ask that you and the poker be blessed with the transformation of all the outworn pain. This pain that you sometimes feel is universal and is calling out to be lifted up and out of your system completely. I have teams of assistance that help me remove old stuck grids that block up your energy system. What has been issued to the surface for release within you lately? This is happening around the globe at high velocity right now so the purging of all that is dark on earth will be released up and out of the earth's surface and completely freed from interfering with your good health, joy and vitality. Do not be afraid of what has caused you pain. Ask me for the transformation of all that is dark and wants to go be released from your system to be purged. For you are pure light my friend. It is time that all of the outdated guilt, grief and traumas be transformed into the Divine Light from which you came. I am here for you and I have your back with all of it. Let the painful triggers - those things that are not the real you - be transformed and you shall be set free."

Notes, inspired writing or other brainstorming ideas...

Day 117 – Archangel Zadkiel

"Your support teams are increasing. We are sending you more energetic assistance. We are your advisory team and anything you need, ask us. It is our job to delegate support, love and help on any level you need it. The frequencies are raising this year for humanity to receive the new templates for peace on earth. You may no longer find feasible what used to give you relief or comfort. This is where we come in… to bring you that extra boost assistance and love from the Divine. Ask and ye shall receive."

Notes, inspired writing or other brainstorming ideas...

Day 118 – Archangel Michael

"What you are being called to do is Divinely guided for you to bring to fruition with your thoughts, your love, your ideas, your gifts. No one else on earth can do this like you can. What have you been guided to do that you have been putting off? If you were given only 3 months to live what would you do? If you absolutely knew how worthy, how gifted, how loved and how supported you are, what would you begin taking action with today? All of the Archangels and myself bring you the energy, supportive frequencies, encouragement and blessings for what you are called to do. There is no one with your exact gifts (which were bestowed to you by the Creator) – you are irreplaceable. Write down what you have felt nudged to do so we may bless this for you and inspire you to take further action with it."

Notes, inspired writing or other brainstorming ideas...

Day 119 – Archangel Chamuel

"We are anchoring strength into all of your chakras and energy bodies today… if you'd like us to, just say Yes and we will begin. We bring you support energy lines to The Divine so that you feel completely connected up and stable. It is now possible to stay strong and secure consistently, with the support system that is now here for you. Feel this fortitude today as you allow the reinforcement from all of the Archangels in."

Notes, inspired writing or other brainstorming ideas...

Day 120 – Archangel Michael

"All the resources you need comes from why you are here. How you are called to make a difference has the power to change everything for not only your life but the lives of everyone on the planet. Why do you want to make a difference in the lives of others? Your inner resources begin with this question. Ponder this question today and I will meet you there… bringing you the inner strength you desire. The emotional lens you see the world through holds within it seeds of creation that have the power to positively impact the lives of 7 plus billion people on the planet. I give you new perceptions (as you ask for my assistance) until you feel unstoppable momentum."

Notes, inspired writing or other brainstorming ideas...

Day 121 – Archangel Jophiel

"Your heart feels the love of all that is most natural. You will be remembered for your service here upon the earth. Let your heart continue leading you to greener playing fields where the sky is blue, the air is refreshing and your heart beats in sync with the beauty felt from within. Follow the river's twists and turns and venture in it for a fun ride of blissful adventures that are sure to bring you all you have been desiring. You are loved and cherished by all of us and the Divine. I am here to assist you with anything you need. What is it you most want? I will be helping you with this. Watch the Universe rearrange blessings for you upon asking for my help. You are worth every blessing that arrives at your doorstep. Be in love with your life, for we are!"

Notes, inspired writing or other brainstorming ideas...

Day 122 – Archangel Michael

"We want to remind you today to please call on our assistance with anything you need help with. We cannot usually come in and help, unless we have your permission. You asking for needed support is vital at this time. The outworn strongholds that do not serve you are shifting loose and you are being connected up to receive more backing and provisions. The love for you is boundless. We want any suffering to end. Ask and ye shall receive. We cannot say that enough times, for it is the truth, more now than ever before."

Notes, inspired writing or other brainstorming ideas...

Day 123 – Archangel Raguel

"We welcome you this new year in peace and gratitude. You have come a long way on your journey, my friend. What you intend tonight… we will be assisting you with. Let the love of your heart fill with the love we hold for you. As you focus on what most pleases you, you uplift the entire globe. Your energy of upliftment does in fact matter. Let what you love be amplified through your heart this evening and what you most want will be anchored into your new year so that all you focus upon takes root much more easily. You have so much love in your heart to give. Let the love uplift you and grow you to new levels of freedom and expansion like you've never experienced before. You are our brothers and sisters and we are with you by your side day and night. May peace bring all your desires into form."

Notes, inspired writing or other brainstorming ideas...

Day 124 – Archangel Michael

"Where there is love, there are seeds of hope. Where there is peace, there is no resistance. Where there is joy, there are many fruitful connections. Global transformation happens in all nations as each individual stops trying to control anything in the outside world they are viewing. How do you feel peace within yourself when you are sensing the releasing of anger and old ways of doing things all over the media? It begins with bringing in light for yourself, your home, your friends and your family. Call upon us, all of The Archangels, to fill your heart with peaceful tones of pure creation itself. See, feel and sense this light filling you, your home, all the people you know and all of the earth. The light of pure creation itself sounds like a peaceful song vibration. Feel this envelop you morning, noon and night. Your heart's harmony brings peace to all people, lands and locations."

Notes, inspired writing or other brainstorming ideas...

Day 125 – Archangel Raziel

"Let today be a brand new start. This is the beginning of your life, right here, right now. Today we bring you frequencies of light for a fresh new start. Soak them up, because what held you back before no longer exists. Let the great beginning you wished for begin now. You are ready and we are lifting your vibration and thoughts to new heights. All you want is available in this moment. Breathe this in deeply into your lungs. And so it is."

Notes, inspired writing or other brainstorming ideas...

Day 126 – Archangel Michael

"You presenting what you believe into the world ushers in additional light to the situation and to the many who are seeking Source Love and strength. When great lights allow themselves to shine it propels others forward to reveal theirs more quickly. The battle has already been won within you. You are giving great fortitude for many who need to stand up and win their own internal wars and claim their freedom. We stand with you today in the strength of my sword cutting away all that is not part of the Divine Source Light that was dragging you down. Feel this connected power anchored within you. If you do not feel it, ask and it shall be given."

Notes, inspired writing or other brainstorming ideas...

Day 127 – Archangel Haniel

"Now is more significant than ever to listen to the inner promptings. It is ever so important to not listen to what the world is telling you to pay attention to or do. Now is a time of tuning into and following what is aligned for your highest and best good. Journaling and asking us questions will assist you because we show you better ways of doing things or changes that need to be made in order to feel more stable and connected from within. Now is the time to sync up to your soul, the Divine and the Archangels more than ever. We are showing you your best course of action through your dreams and inner guidance system. Ask us questions and you will know the answers within a day or two."

Notes, inspired writing or other brainstorming ideas...

Day 128 – Archangel Michael

"When you know you are aligned to your inner calling, the promptings from within will become like vibrant whispers shining a light in the direction of the sun. How do you know which choices to say yes to? What pulls you forward and strengthens you is for the good of all. What feels like an obsession, yet drains your energy or depletes you may not be the choice that will bring you the ultimate peace, joy and clarity. Your desires will always be there. The yearnings that help you grow your tree roots deeper will bring you the momentum you are seeking."

Notes, inspired writing or other brainstorming ideas...

Day 129 – Archangel Metatron

"If you'd like to receive more assistance with your life's work, call upon me to enhance your life path. I will deliver to you a sacred geometry blueprint of higher understanding of your soul's purpose. Placed in your heart, you'll feel a sweetness and magical unfolding that will occur in your life with almost effortless flow. If you would like this, I bring this to you today and while you sleep, in alignment with Divine Will. This aligns you to a higher understanding of how to flow in sync with the Golden Divine Light placed around the earth by me and all of the Archangels. When you are in unison with this golden light, Divine Flow will bring you the most pleasant and supportive gifts. This will occur naturally as you ask for my assistance and align to the Divine Will for the planet. We thank you for your reception and open heartedness to serve and be the love that you already are. Through grace and love all things are possible."

Notes, inspired writing or other brainstorming ideas...

Day 130 – Archangel Michael

"Doubters often doubt the nature of their own existence. When you encounter someone who is negative towards you and questions something you hold dear to your heart, this is a signal to trust yourself even more, not less. We have your back. We will not let you fall. When you feel knocked around by life, ask us to carry you to higher ground and show you how things can be easier, for they really can. We are always by your side the instant you think of us."

Notes, inspired writing or other brainstorming ideas...

Day 131 – Archangel Daniel

"We are shining our light upon you ever so brightly today. Like a lighthouse in the dark of the night, your light shines for many. As you rest, we keep your light house bright for you. All you need to do today is simply request what you'd like assistance with and bathe in Divine Light as we sing you many lullabies. Even the ocean rests its currents when the tide is low. Allow our love to refill your heart all the way full… then before you know it a grand new adventure begins again."

Notes, inspired writing or other brainstorming ideas...

Day 132 – Archangel Michael

"Pray to Divine Mother for blessings for anything that ails you. She is not only a mender of all suffering for humanity, she is an epic healer who removes the weeds of pain in the hearts of those who have been suffering their entire lives. Call upon her before you sleep to lift the suffering from your heart by morning. Her wisdom and great power can remove the suffering of anyone who calls to her. When you are graced by her presence, know that she is real and this is not just a figment of your imagination. Your alignment to Divine Mother anchors in light code treasures for all."

Notes, inspired writing or other brainstorming ideas...

Day 133 – Archangel Ariel

"Whirlwinds of rapid change are now occurring with more intense speeds. There is nothing that can keep you stuck any longer. You have the ability to call in anything you desire, want or need. You have an incredible window of opportunity right now to transform the outwork fears, doubts and angst into a life of connection, love and happiness. Anchor yourself in our love for you today. Feel us send love through your heart, energizing you into a peaceful state. Your light knows your true worthiness. Allow your heart to be open to receive our love. Be as carefree as a butterfly and the winds of transformation will bring you many blessings."

Notes, inspired writing or other brainstorming ideas...

Day 134 — Archangel Michael

"When in doubt rest it out and ask us to bring you inspired thoughts with new options. Anything you'd like is available for you. What brings you the feeling you are soaring through the air on a hang glider or dream you are flying with your arms spread open wide by your intentions of where to go next? There are passageways of light we have anchored on earth that make this easier for you now. What's available are golden light pathways that lift you higher above the troubles and ascends you into the exact place in time you have been dreaming of. Ask us to place you in these golden safety nets of light where what you wish for is manifested by thought and the old simply falls away and transforms. This is the fresh way manifestation is available now. We extend our hand to lift you into all you have ever wanted, for what your heart has longed for is within the Divine Golden Light and blessed by us."

Notes, inspired writing or other brainstorming ideas...

Day 135 - Archangel Raphael

"Your inner resources for healing, abundance, and wisdom are vast. Your connection to your inner light can indeed heal anything that ails you. When you are united passionately to the source within, your authentic power grows. Your health and life improve from this alliance. We bring you radiance from within today, igniting you to be the full blaze of your brilliance. Feel our luminosity linking you up again and be at peace in knowing you are infinitely loved."

Notes, inspired writing or other brainstorming ideas...

Day 136 – Archangel Michael

"You are so loved. You are here to reach the highest level of light you can receive so that others can embody it too. You are worthy, you always have been. You are loved infinitely by me, always and forever. Reach for me. Call upon me to heal any feelings of separateness or pain, for they are not real. I am real and when you are one with me all pain and suffering are transformed into pure light."

Notes, inspired writing or other brainstorming ideas...

Day 137 – Archangel Chamuel

"You are energizing many nations to come to peace when you allow your happiness in. What brings you peace the most? Become one with this today. It has a reverberating effect through the core of Mother Earth and to the other side of her. Let simple pleasures steal your day."

Notes, inspired writing or other brainstorming ideas...

Day 138 – Archangel Michael

"Blessings abound. Let your heart's desire be known to us. That is why we are here, to assist you with bringing your dreams to fruition. Your innermost wishes are blessed by us and the Divine. Climbing your mountain is much easier as you take moments in your day to pause and ask for our love, blessings and support. More viable pathways are shown to you as you do. We love you infinitely and forever."

Notes, inspired writing or other brainstorming ideas...

Day 139 – Archangel Raphael

"What would raise your joy level up a notch today, this week? Waves of healing frequencies are being sent to the earth by all of the Archangels. We are increasing these healing tones right now so that it gives you a boost of support and upliftment that you have been seeking. Making one tiny change to increase your joy quotient brings healing to all. Keep shifting to more happiness and avenues of possibility that have felt impossible before will continue opening up to you. You are loved dearly by all of us."

Notes, inspired writing or other brainstorming ideas...

Day 140 – Archangel Michael

"There is a light source you can always tune into for love, guidance, protection, support and deep connection. Call upon me to help you feel the Divine Light from which you came. Your resilience is strong when you are in the Divine flow of the most sustaining love you can imagine. The love within the flame of the Divine will never let you down. Your connection to Divine Light is infinite and boundless. You are held and rocked at the heart of the Divine today. For this loving consistent presence infinitely has you wrapped in blankets of love always and forever."

Notes, inspired writing or other brainstorming ideas...

Day 141 – Archangel Raphael

"Never hesitate when that burning desire in your soul won't let your dream go. Take the first step. Pretty soon you'll be flying across the sky and all the wind will be lifting you higher."

Notes, inspired writing or other brainstorming ideas...

Day 142 — Archangel Michael

"There is nothing to fear. You have what it takes. When you feel in a bind, call upon me to help you untangle what is not for your highest and best good, for this is my specialty. Unraveling what is "illusion" or feels off and what is "truth for you" and feels joyful is what I help you with. The moment you see the illusion you are free. Be at peace in knowing just how supported you are."

Notes, inspired writing or other brainstorming ideas...

Day 143 – Archangel Azrael

"Celebrate the unknown. Light the fire from within. It is in the unknown that new sparks of passion and creativity are lit up like wild fires. Ride the wind currents… see where they take you. What your heart longs for will be revealed through each twist and turn. Let it be the most magnificent ride ever!"

Notes, inspired writing or other brainstorming ideas...

Day 144 – Archangel Michael

"Vibrant waves of light are being brought into the earth at this time. We thank you for being willing to transform what no longer serves your true happiness path. What you wish for will come true as you joyously bless and release all that holds you back. Get ready for an exuberant ride because it is about to get really, really good for you. Trust, have faith and know I am always here for you."

Notes, inspired writing or other brainstorming ideas...

Day 145 – Archangel Gabriel

"You have circled the globe and back in search of many things, even if just on the internet or in your connections with others online. You have discovered it is all about LOVE. What you have been searching for all along is that deepest possible love you can feel on earth and you have realized you already have it. All of the love of the cosmos is contained within one atom within You. Everything you reach for is here now and can burst forth from your heart at any moment in order to be one with all that is and ever was. You ARE it. We love you to infinity and beyond."

Notes, inspired writing or other brainstorming ideas...

Day 146 – Archangel Michael

"Trust the words you are being guided to speak. Saying words you do not really feel as valid for you create an incongruence within your higher connection channels that actually blocks the flow from higher realms from flooding your entire being with greater wisdom than you could possibly imagine. Call upon me to help your words be congruent with how you ultimately feel. If this is not something you normally feel safe in doing, this will be so good for you on a soul level to practice. We surround you with our light as you align to your truth, your heart and your desires through Divine Love."

Notes, inspired writing or other brainstorming ideas...

Day 147 – Archangel Uriel

"Think about the areas of your life, work or projects you'd like us to energize today. Write 5 of your dreams down. We bring them blessings from the Angelic Realm today and tonight while you sleep. Also, write down any worries or unforgiveness that you want us to help release and transform. The second you ask we begin working diligently on your behalf. It is our honor to do so. The strength of all of the angels are with you this day and forevermore."

Notes, inspired writing or other brainstorming ideas...

Day 148 — Archangel Michael

"We are flooding you with light beams of goodness right now. As you tune into our love for you, what you previously thought was impossible is made real. Viable solutions and ideas spring forth as you celebrate the journey right where you are. We bring you ideas on a silver platter today as you ask us for assistance with anything in your life you want to elevate. New horizons will show up for you. You are not forgotten. Ask for a sign and we will bring one specifically for you that you'll indeed recognize."

Notes, inspired writing or other brainstorming ideas...

Day 149 – Archangel Gabriel

"We bathe you today in the light of how much you are loved, cherished and adored. Sometimes it seems we are very far away, but we are not, we are right by your side. Let yourself rest easily today and bask in the feeling of soft rose petals all around you. Enjoy the purity and goodness we bring you and the fullness of those gifts that will blossom at the right time."

Notes, inspired writing or other brainstorming ideas...

Day 150 — Archangel Michael

"All you dream of is more than possible. To manifest what you are desiring through the higher 5th dimensional golden light grids (which are now all around the earth) is as simple as feeling yourself already there. Being one with your creations and asking that they be aligned to Divine Will brings them through. Have patience. This process of creating through 5th dimensional Divine Light will get easier as you play with it and dance your ideas into form."

Notes, inspired writing or other brainstorming ideas . . .

Day 151 – Archangel Gabriel

"Your perspective is important and DOES matter. You have arrived at the exact place in time where all you desire can be born through you. The obstacles and old shackles have been removed. What do you most want? I, Gabriel will help you with this. Write this down and all of the Archangels, including myself will be rolling up our sleeves to assist you with this in every way possible. Be at peace and visualize this coming to be."

Notes, inspired writing or other brainstorming ideas...

Day 152 – Archangel Michael

"You are allowed to change your mind at any time. When we give you a higher blueprint of what may work better, this can alter once brought into physical form. We are always working with you to find what may work better. Ask for an upgraded version of the blueprint at any time. This will help prevent you from getting stuck in one way of doing things. There usually is a more fun, enjoyable way of going about things that we can bring you."

Notes, inspired writing or other brainstorming ideas...

Day 153 – Archangel Zadkiel

"Naysayers are usually not freedom fighters at all costs. The limitations they see are the bars they have built up in their own minds for themselves. When someone is negative towards what you are doing, take it as a sign that you have moved beyond extensive limitations from within yourself. What you are being guided to do, be or have is specifically unique for your soul's calling which has nothing to do with appeasing other's doubts or fears. You didn't come here to bar yourself up, you came here to fly like a freedom dove in the bluest skies of all."

Notes, inspired writing or other brainstorming ideas...

Day 154 – Archangel Michael

"In the midst of chaos, call upon me to help you keep the peace. You are tremendously treasured for diligently seeking to bring more peace to your world. Support IS here for you. Every step of the way we ARE available. We bring you your favorite flowers to focus upon when you are feeling off center. Rest and rejuvenate. For all is well."

Notes, inspired writing or other brainstorming ideas...

Day 155 – Archangel Uriel

"As cycles come to an end, the road ahead looks smoother for many. The angelic realms are bringing through frequencies to the planet that carry with them the birthing of many new ideas, creations, inventions and improvements. Call upon us to help you anchor in your creative ideas into form… for they are very much needed for the expansion and upliftment of the entire earth. When you receive a new idea, something that lights you up, do not disregard this, see how you can play with it and let it speak to you. Let our light shine upon your expansion ideas, for they will be given wings by us as you do. You are in the flow of what your soul came here to do as you bring through your upgraded soul purpose blueprints."

Notes, inspired writing or other brainstorming ideas...

Day 156 – Archangel Michael

"You have what it takes and then some. Be willing to ask for more help. Be open. Smile and laugh all the petty stuff off. This time in your life is supposed to get easier and will. Your ideas are a hit, keep going. Make em' laugh. Make em' smile. Let your natural talent shine through. This is your time to shine. We are shining our light upon you and your creations all through the day and night. You got this."

Notes, inspired writing or other brainstorming ideas...

Day 157 – Archangel Gabriel

"You are universally connected to all that is and ever was. You play a vital part in humanity's awakening as you ask to reawaken within you your true source of power and enter into the light from which you came. That which is never ending, never beginning… always love, always supportive, always connecting you to the greater part of yourself. When worry enters your mind with any obstacles, call upon us the Archangels and Ganesh to assist you with removing them. We work as a team and it is our honor to join you up to your authentic empowerment source… The Divine, all the way, so that the obstacles fade as the distortion dissipates into love… into truth. Let love wash away self-doubt. Let your heart be bathed in liquid-golden-love today by saying, Yes, I receive all the Love from The Divine that's waiting for me."

Notes, inspired writing or other brainstorming ideas . . .

Day 158 – Archangel Michael

"You are hearing the call correctly. We are showing you invigorating worlds of possibility today that bring with them the joy you have been longing for. You understand how to receive well the inner guidance we are bringing to you in each moment. Allow the sun to rise again, for this is a new day in your life of creation. The seeds of opportunity are now springing into creative form now, awaiting your enjoyment to the fullest."

Notes, inspired writing or other brainstorming ideas...

Day 159 – Archangel Raziel

"Just wait… more joy is coming. It only gets better from here as we bring you inexhaustible possibilities. You are a team player. You are listening to the inner promptings exquisitely. Doors of filled celebration swing wide open with all the appreciation in that beautiful heart of yours. What awaits you is the greatest love of all. Cheers to you tuning into each moment…feeling the whispers of guidance we bring you. Your path is genuinely bright indeed."

Notes, inspired writing or other brainstorming ideas...

Day 160 – Archangel Michael

"Saying no doesn't have to mean you are selfish or 'not nice'. When you feel something is not right for you, we'd like you to tune into this even more, amplify it. What rings true for others may not ring a bell for you. Your alignment to your Soul and the Divine will feel like Divine Flow for you. When something comes in energetically that feels like a cog in your wheel, ask me to assist you. It is my specialty to remove disturbing energies from entering your sacred space. Being assertively in your authentic power is what we want for you. If others have ideas about what you may be able to deliver for them or bring them, yet you feel "out of sorts" by their demands upon your time or energy, we advise you to listen to these feelings very closely. Being in your authentic power doesn't mean to submit to others wishes in order to appease the crowd. The real you - your soul - knows the bigger picture. Your soul does not want you to feel comfortable with that which is not for your highest and best good. Discomfort always comes from being out of alignment with self. Alignment to what your Divine Flow is brings peace, ease of being, sweetness and a feeling of safety as you move forward with inspired ideas."

Notes, inspired writing or other brainstorming ideas...

Day 161 – Archangel Metatron

"Long ago you chose to come into this time space reality you call Now to brighten the days of others and be the bright flame that you are in the night's darkest whispers of the hour. Much transformation is taking place within you at this time. You are ready. You have not been forgotten. Once long ago you made a decision to come to earth to experience the pleasure of it. In this lifetime as you allow yourself to experience the Divine Design of Mother Earth and become one with her heartbeat while basking in blissful nature moments, you break loose the old strongholds that once held you back. Once all these old shells are transformed out of your system, your flame will never be dampened again while you walk this earth for the rest of your life. There have been a lot of trials along the way, but we congratulate you today, for you have made it back home."

Notes, inspired writing or other brainstorming ideas...

Day 162 – Archangel Michael

"Rest assured you are not doing this alone. Your students are our students – those that learn from you we are assisting on the inner dimensions of light. You have an entire room full of Angels there with you when you are imparting your wisdom to others. Celebrate the joys of those "lightbulb" moments you see happen in those you are sharing ideas with. In these lit up segments we bring everyone who is near seeds of goodwill and light codes of happiness from The Divine and all of the Angels. This expansion is long lasting. Enjoying these moments as long as possible allows us to deliver you and all whom you love, precious seeds of wisdom and life giving sustenance from the Divine Creator. Riding the bliss currents helps us usher in love, protection and strength to the masses. Herein lies the secret of a lifetime of extended happiness through the healing and support that is always available for you."

Notes, inspired writing or other brainstorming ideas...

Day 163 – Archangel Gabriel

"You bring peace to the hearts of many. Your ideas are being anointed today with our love. What do you wish you were doing in the world that you hold yourself back from? Place this on a crystal plate in your mind's eye for us to bless. As you do this we are activating this area of your life today, so that which has held you back dissipates and is replaced with clarity of purpose. There is no better time for this than now. Go forth and let the world see your bright and shining eyes and smile. We reach out our hand to yours because what comes next is more joy, sweet tenderness and love's embrace."

Notes, inspired writing or other brainstorming ideas...

Day 164 – Archangel Michael

"There is no need to rush through any more parts of your life. What helps you most is to be easy about it. We assure you what we are guiding you to do, be and experience will happen with ease and grace by surrendering any need to control the outcomes. You are a treasured, delicate and brave soul upon the earth. Walking through the fear to the other side brings rainbows of peace for all. Set your eyes upon what you would prefer to see, instead of letting the frightening parts hold you up. Let the wind breathe underneath your wings and have fun with some test flights. Your wings love the practice for the experience of it. Savored creative journeys bring happiness to your heart and soul. Allow the whirlwind of love to be the ascension points for flying into horizons that are calling your name. I will be there for you to ensure your safe flight."

Notes, inspired writing or other brainstorming ideas...

Day 165 – Archangel Ariel

"Be sure to not beat yourself up over the little things. Your higher self, your soul is already all you wish to be in the world. Be wise with your time, but don't cramp your style with placing too much on your precious plate in one day's serving. This causes constriction in your body, mind and heart. Allow for white space in your day and enjoy the fluffy brilliant clouds that sing praises to you. We are in the clouds smiling, waving and watching you. You can take the pressure off now. All is unfolding in the ideal Diving Timing for your soul."

Notes, inspired writing or other brainstorming ideas...

Day 166 – Archangel Michael

"You are the new young one in town. You have arrived, our friend. Cherish each moment in the here and now. There is nothing ahead you need to speed to arrive at. What will make the most impact in your life is to be fully present with each moment, every person you encounter and every glorious sunset. What's ahead may seem daunting at times, but we assure you that you ARE capable. Be that which you came to be, YOU. You already are enough. Letting go of pleasing others who are not aligned to your Divine Destiny or the highest and best good of all will set your heart free for the rest of your life. Never are you asked to give more than feels good to. Saying enough is enough makes your heart sing again. Just ahead to greet you are choirs of angels singing for the freedom that is yours. You deserve this and more."

Notes, inspired writing or other brainstorming ideas...

Day 167 – Archangel Zadkiel

"When you get downtrodden on yourself remember that this earth school is not easy. You knew before you came here nothing about it was going to be easy at first. You knew you were going to have to learn the ropes. Let yourself off the hook from having to please anyone. It is in the receiving of all that is good in your life that more joy, happiness, longevity and tender sweet moments open up to you like an angelic, fuchsia-filled cloud sunset. You have done more than your fair share for now. Let each moment be enough. Simply enjoy. Joy raises the entire planet higher. All that you are asked to do at this point is to be the joy that you already are. We are with you in the clouds as you watch us dance in them before your eyes. Cheers to your being-ness."

Notes, inspired writing or other brainstorming ideas...

Day 168 – Archangel Michael

"Bring love into the equation. Through heartfelt love and compassion all things are possible. We sing praises for you today. What you have created is far greater than the eye can see. You have sown hope into the hearts of many. Be proud our dear friend, you have done well in the eyes of your Divine Mother and Father. Your ideas and creations have not gone unnoticed. Continue forth. We cheer you on. Enjoy every last drop. Rest assured you have done well."

Notes, inspired writing or other brainstorming ideas...

Day 169 – Archangel Gabriel

"Be willing to get it wrong. That's how you learn where your Divine Flow is. Trust what works, let go of what doesn't. Write your ideas and thoughts down. All of them matter. Write from your heart what moves you. Pinpoint entrapments. Tell the story from different vantage points. Let yourself be heard. What you have to say will help save many lives. Honor the written word, spoken through you. Create a movement. Let yourself be known."

Notes, inspired writing or other brainstorming ideas...

Day 170 — Archangel Michael

"Honoring yourself with what feels absolutely good for you, heals the soul. You are never asked to go beyond what would feel "off" to you. Let those situations, people, places and things go that drag you down. Your authentic smile that glimmers a thousand miles is what your soul wishes for you. Nothing more, nothing less. Your happiness is the end goal. Your heart filled with rose blossoms of love is the end all. Did you know your smile holds the light frequencies to heal the someone who has lost seemingly everything? Yes indeed, we bring upliftment for all through your genuine smile. Therein lies the secret. It's all within your heart-smiles."

Notes, inspired writing or other brainstorming ideas...

Day 171 — Archangel Ariel

"Trust that everything is going to be okay. You are making the right decisions at the right time. What needed to happen is happening now. Take time out to recover and heal all the tender layers. You are worth this time out period. Now is the moment to give to yourself; recharge your batteries. You are teaching by example here. Nurture you, the stars are in your favor for this. Be willing to let go of all the superfluous. Allow Divine Mother to feed you, comfort you and show you the way. You are Divine by nature and you deserve the sweetest affections."

Notes, inspired writing or other brainstorming ideas...

Day 172 – Archangel Michael

"Heal that which you came here to heal. Sometimes those who trigger the most pain within you are those you are meant to be released fully from on an energetic level in this lifetime and previous ones. Those who don't understand you are the ones in the most pain and suffering internally, although they may not let you know this. These ones need the most releasing from your system because if there is a pain point within you, you can be sure there is one within them. Archangel Raphael and I work as a team to heal this for you. Ask us for this deep disappointment to be healed within you and them completely. You will notice a releasing happening within you. Rest assured this is being healed across the timeline, in other lifetimes as well. You are worth peace and peace shall be yours."

Notes, inspired writing or other brainstorming ideas...

Day 173 – Archangel Ariel

"When you are drawn to say no to someone, do. This is honoring yourself and the other. There is no need to suffer for the sake of not wanting to hurt someone's feelings. The other person usually needs to know how their behavior is affecting others. When someone is unaware of how they may be negatively affecting those around them, sometimes loving but firm boundaries are the only way they learn a higher way of being. When you say no, also ask Archangel Michael to cut cordings for you from them to you and you to them. This way there is no lingering guilt or manipulative energy that causes you to do things not for your highest and best good. Releasing yourself from these burdens helps all involved and also helps Mother Earth release her burdens as well. You are given permission to say no. In a lot of cases it is a very kind thing to do."

Notes, inspired writing or other brainstorming ideas . . .

Day 174 — Archangel Michael

"Where there is love there is unification and purification. Love feels the truth. Love arranges circumstances around as naturally as a butterflies' wings gliding in the sunset breeze. The love of you knows this unforced way of being. We invite you to enter the circle of effortless Divine flow with all of us Archangels today. You are safe to spread your wings and glide like an Eagle into the electric blue horizon of new beginnings."

Notes, inspired writing or other brainstorming ideas...

Day 175 – Archangel Uriel

"What reveals itself to you in plain view (that which is obviously trying to get your attention) is our way of stopping you in your tracks to get your attention sometimes. The tender arms of Divine Mother reach out to you today to help you know that the struggle no longer needs to be so. Where there is pain, there is healing waiting to wrap you in wings of love. Where there is neglect of self, lack of love from within, there is liquid golden love to refill the dark voids. Where there is anger at self there are sweet honeysuckle flowers waiting for you to bathe in the sunlight with them. Let us gift you with the absolute Divine Love frequencies you are most needing to counterbalance the ill effects of any self rejection, disappointment and regret that may be buried deep inside. Name your feelings and we will anoint you with the antidote healing balms of divinity you most need right now. It is in the asking that you shall receive."

Notes, inspired writing or other brainstorming ideas...

Day 176 – Archangel Michael

"Divine Mother wants you to receive your heart's desires. Dance, play and commune with her as often as possible as you get in touch with the purity that is you. She will enhance your God given right to receive what is for your highest and best good and clear the pathway for you with evergreen grace."

Notes, inspired writing or other brainstorming ideas...

Day 177 — Archangel Gabriel

"Loss of Hope brings great longing to the heart. When you feel sadness, doubt and insecurity take this as a very good sign. It means you are ready to shed the old self protection mechanisms. Those areas of your life that are in desperate need of transformation are coming to the surface to be lifted up and out of your energy bodies, your auric field. Sometimes it feels like previous insecurities and fears might happen again. Please call upon us as this feeling occurs. In doing so we will be there to deliver you new thought forms of the heaven on earth that's available for you now. Be willing for it to get really, really good. You deserve the Divine Magic that's at your door."

Notes, inspired writing or other brainstorming ideas...

Day 178 – Archangel Michael

"You deserve for your life to feel like "heaven on earth". What works for some may not function well in your world. Where is your favorite location on earth? What feeling does that location bring you? You deserve this feeling in your everyday life. Take the struggle of your life and place it into a pink ball of light and hand it to Mother Mary. She is here today as a bringer of peace and deliverer of love. Mother Mary in turn gifts you with a white present wrapped in a golden ribbon that has your name written on it. Receive your present in through your heart chakra and feel, sense or see what your gift is from Mother Mary."

Notes, inspired writing or other brainstorming ideas...

Day 179 — Archangel Raphael

"This being the time of the great Ascension means that it is also a time you may be feeling the upsets of the world in your own energy system. When you wake up on the wrong side of the bed do not blame yourself. Call upon me to bathe you in my emerald light beams. It is my specialty to help your body, mind and soul be whole again. When you are having trouble letting go of other people's thoughts and wishes for your life that don't feel good to you, call me in. I will remove their energies from your light body and deliver it back to their soul with healing intact. Any pains you have will be healed by the light of the Divine through me. You no longer need to carry the burdens of others around. The Ascension on earth for humans means it is time for all beings to be free of the darker energies that once had taken over this planet. Your time of ascension into who you really are, at a Soul level, is here. Be that which you are and allow us to transform all that is not you. In doing so you will feel as expanded and light as a dove flying free from its cage of captivity."

Notes, inspired writing or other brainstorming ideas...

Day 180 — Archangel Michael

"You are ready for the love of the century to run through your veins. You have been waiting for eons of time to receive this expansion of love light that naturally dissipates false illusion and fear. Now is your time. These light codes of love we send you have freedom wings and infinity at their reach. This love hawk lifts you above the bluest oceans into the dawn of a new day. Cheers to the love that is already you."

Notes, inspired writing or other brainstorming ideas...

Day 181 — Archangel Haniel

"The love for you runs deeper than the farthest Universe imaginable. Your heart beating right now is a sure sign of how much you are loved. Rest easy, in peace today knowing how much you are taken care of. Your gift for humanity is to love who you are completely and through that love the flowers that blossom are here to show you how uplifting life can be for you. We celebrate with you today as you let your thoughts be easy on yourself. Beautiful unfoldings are in the works for your life in miraculous ways. We love you."

Notes, inspired writing or other brainstorming ideas...

Day 182 — Archangel Michael

"You are celebrated beyond belief for tuning into yourself so much that the obstacles keep turning into stepping stones. Your heartfelt desire to be in a state of creation with all that is paves the way for many blessings to come. Learning what will work better for you creates a ripple effect in the Universe of infinite possibilities to enter your world and uplift the lives of others. You are capable of everything you set out to do, be and experience. There are many blessings headed your way through the creation process of inspired ideas that are here for you."

Notes, inspired writing or other brainstorming ideas...

Day 183 – Archangel Raphael

"The love you give yourself has the power to heal a hundred nations. Trust that you are on the right track when you look inwards for guidance, love, nurturance and surrender. What do you most want this year? Place this on a silver platter for us to bless. You deserve the peace that this will bring, our dear friend. What you wish for will bless not only your life, but the entire planet and infinite universes."

Notes, inspired writing or other brainstorming ideas . . .

Day 184 — Archangel Michael

"Stay true to your inner joy promptings. When you get an insight of more love, happiness, or heart connection run with it. All of us are supporting you on it. You are an inspiration for the world as you implement your ideas into action. Even if you feel your creations aren't worth anything, they are indeed! Call upon us to energize them for you. We will help show you the highest and best path for you to take. It's all right here, now. Sometimes it requires more light brought in for you to see things clearly. That's where we come in - all of the Archangels. What you desire is possible. Go forth and be one with your ideas with us. This will bring life to them beyond your wildest imagination. Always at your service."

Notes, inspired writing or other brainstorming ideas...

Day 185 – Archangel Ariel

"We are celebrating with you today. For the fresh changes are already ushering in positive new energy for you and all whom you touch, and will be uplifting with your message and life. Your Joy is contagious. There are only great things to come for you. You are in alignment to receive it all. Have fun most of all and just allow the unfoldings to occur at their natural pace. Many pleasant surprises await. Your life is a grand adventure and we are applauding your bravery."

Notes, inspired writing or other brainstorming ideas...

Day 185 – Archangel Ariel

"We are celebrating with you today. For the fresh changes are already ushering in positive new energy for you and all whom you touch, and will be uplifting with your message and life. Your Joy is contagious. There are only great things to come for you. You are in alignment to receive it all. Have fun most of all and just allow the unfoldings to occur at their natural pace. Many pleasant surprises await. Your life is a grand adventure and we are applauding your bravery."

Notes, inspired writing or other brainstorming ideas...

Day 186 – Archangel Michael

"We are energizing those areas of your life you have felt were missing for quite some time so that more joy is activated within you. This causes a ripple effect with all of your connections, projects and creations. Ask yourself today what you'd like more of... could just be a feeling. Allow us to bring you more energy, ideas, love and connection for these areas you have missed in your life. More often in your life you'll feel the sparks from within lighting up with synergy . You are a grand creator and we support your inner most longings and ideas for new creations. We love you endlessly and beyond."

Notes, inspired writing or other brainstorming ideas...

Day 187 – Archangel Jeremiel

"Enjoy your day fully. There is sweet pure love waiting for you. It is our honor to send it to you. We are pleased to see when you are smiling. The Divine has unending upliftment for you and we are always available to bring you these higher frequencies of being. Request and you shall receive in delightful ways."

Notes, inspired writing or other brainstorming ideas...

Day 188 – Archangel Michael

"Healing happens when you are inclined to let go of the strong holds and tango with the wispy winds of transformation that are here for you. We delight in watching your heart smiles of new beginnings and enchanted journeys of the soul. What once was hard is made easy as you hold out your hand for the sweetest loved-filled dance of all. We meet you there at eternities door, igniting within you the lightness of sun-filled clouds on a picnic afternoon."

Notes, inspired writing or other brainstorming ideas...

Day 189 – Archangel Raphael

"You have made it across the threshold. Get ready for a very fun adventure coming your way. Your diligence of releasing what no longer serves you has made room for all the goodness the Universe has waiting for you to arrive sweetly at your doorstep. You will be pleasantly surprised. We are always available upon request."

Notes, inspired writing or other brainstorming ideas...

Day 190 – Archangel Michael

"You are stronger than you think. Admitting what you want doesn't have to be scary. Help is on board with ALL that you think about. Those that receive what they want are willing to keep trying 100 ways to allow it to show up for them. They do not doubt it will arrive. They know without a shadow of a doubt how much they are supported with their desires. You are too. We have your back with 1000 angel wings. Feel this in your heart today. Our love is your love."

Notes, inspired writing or other brainstorming ideas...

Day 191 — Archangel Gabriel

"You are doing a spectacular job connecting to the more of you. You are a dancing delight to watch expand. You have the ability and the momentum to bring to fruition the ideas you have been thinking about. All of the Universe is conspiring to assist you in every way possible. As you tune in you can feel that support with every breath you take. We are celebrating you today and holding up a toast in your honor."

Notes, inspired writing or other brainstorming ideas...

Day 192 — Archangel Michael

"When the world shakes you up trust that you are well supported by legions of angels. Call upon us daily. Energy grid systems that no longer need to be there are shaking loose as cycles in your life come to a close. Ask me to remove these old energy patterns that no longer serve you or what you have come to the planet to do. Your higher frequencies of light are anchoring in as the outdated is being transformed. Let the clearing run deep, for what comes next is better than expected."

Notes, inspired writing or other brainstorming ideas...

Day 193 – Archangel Gabriel

"Life is full of twists and turns. What you really want in your heart is possible. Call upon me to help point you in the direction of your answered prayers. You are worthy of all of your dreams unfolding in this lifetime. Ask me to help you with the highest and best version of your heart's longing, for I will bring helpers into your life so that this unfolds in alignment with your Soul's Purpose. Be free and have fun most of all, for when you are singing so are we. We love you."

Notes, inspired writing or other brainstorming ideas...

Day 194 – Archangel Michael

"We are sending you our light of strength today, so you may feel supported and strengthened with Divine Light through your central channel, around you, all the way through the center of the earth and up to the Divine. We want you to feel us holding you in this light of strength, love, clarity and protection. Be easy on yourself, for you are doing a great job. You are enough and are being gently guided to all that is for your highest and best good. You don't have to be strong yourself, we've got you. Let our angel wings wrap around you and soak up our fortitude that's always here for you."

Notes, inspired writing or other brainstorming ideas...

Day 195 – Archangel Ariel

"When in doubt, ask us to assist you with letting go of anything draining your energy. We will help you release or transform those areas no longer serving your highest and best interest at this time. You are worthy of all that would make your heart sing with joy. The life your heart desires is within reach. By letting go of energy drains on your system we help you make room for better options… more vibrant choices that fill you with peace and put a smile on your face every day."

Notes, inspired writing or other brainstorming ideas...

Day 196 – Archangel Michael

"Freedom begins with a no nonsense approach for the truth. Truth has a vibration, a tone. It resonates in the heart as chimes of happiness or resounding waves of clarity. When you know something is true your energy bodies chime together in unison (sometimes with truth goosebumps) to let you know what you've heard you can heed. When you know, you know. When something is right for you, all of you feels the bells of clarity go off. When in doubt wait it out. Clarity can be found in moment to moment listening. In the listening you will know."

Notes, inspired writing or other brainstorming ideas...

Day 197 – Archangel Metatron

"Celebrate the joy that arrives. Relish the good fortune that is here for you. More is coming. It has been a long and treacherous journey indeed. You have navigated the hills well, my friend. What seemed like would never happen is made available to you now. You have the blessings of all the stars upon you. Joy is here to stay. Rest assured, you are home inside now."

Notes, inspired writing or other brainstorming ideas...

Day 198 – Archangel Michael

"Nurturing the love that is here for you helps you move beyond previously set limitations you may have placed on yourself. The love of you knows that all is well. What feels scary will prove to be worth moving past your comfort zone and once you do, the freedom flight that follows will lift you with grace to the bluest skies of all."

Notes, inspired writing or other brainstorming ideas...

Day 199 – Archangel Chamuel

"Divine assistance is here for you in immense ways. Where do you want us to flow blessings in your life? Think of these areas today. Picture Golden Light enveloping you and flooding the parts of your life you want help with the most. When Golden Light, which is Divine Will, fills your central channel, your body, mind, soul and your projects, obstacles are removed from behind the scenes, making your manifesting process much easier. It is our honor to assist you with this today and every day."

Notes, inspired writing or other brainstorming ideas...

Day 200 – Archangel Michael

"You come from infinite Love. What we bring you is the remembering of that which you already are. When you doubt that you are deserving of Love and all that is good for you, you separate yourself from the source of infinite Love. You separate yourself from the whole of you. It is through Love you are healed. Let your eyes look in the mirror today and see only Love."

Notes, inspired writing or other brainstorming ideas...

Day 201 – Archangel Gabriel

"Deep longing is a good sign. Your desires reveal to you that which your soul is trying to get you in touch with. Sometimes these voids are filled with substitutes that do not match the frequency of what you are actually craving. We stream light beams of love frequencies to you today to fill these empty areas up with the Divine Light your soul has been calling you to do. Allow the worry, sorrow and feelings of lack of love be filled up with golden and violet beams of Source Light. Now is the time to refuse any substitutes. For what you are truly craving is the Divine Essence of who you are returned back to the center of you in whole form."

Notes, inspired writing or other brainstorming ideas...

Day 202 — Archangel Michael

"What opens your heart up like blossoming wild flowers expands the hearts of others. Honoring all parts of yourself by speaking what works better for you helps those around you be more of their authentic selves. Your alignment to your true self matters. Loving your quirks makes you – you. We honor today those parts of yourself you have wanted to keep hidden. The bright star within is ready to blaze a trail for all parts of you to merge with your star-flamed soul. As it does, your light can never be dimmed again. We adore the real you. We celebrate with you today as swirls of Divine light give you a Cosmic hug."

Notes, inspired writing or other brainstorming ideas...

Day 203 — Archangel Uriel

"Deep within you is a reservoir of aliveness. This is where your fountain of youth is. Today we help you tap this cosmic well spring that recharges all of your energy systems with renewal frequencies. This purification process is available for you to transform the heaviness (all that is not you) into light. We spin Divine Golden Light around you (at your request) that purifies worries into Cosmic fuel. This Cosmic light, which is aligned to Divine Will, sparks up desires you never knew you had. As you release concerns of your heart into this spinning Golden Light, we alchemize what is no longer serving your highest and best interest into all your heart has dreamed for and more."

Notes, inspired writing or other brainstorming ideas...

Day 204 – Archangel Michael

"When you hop on the train of your Life's Purpose and Soul's Calling the train takes you places you never thought you'd go. Be willing for an adventuresome ride. We are overseeing the train for you. Sometimes the ride will be like gentle sightseeing of ancient times gone by and other hours it will be like a roller coaster ride at Disneyland. Enjoy the ride of the day and know we have your back either way."

Notes, inspired writing or other brainstorming ideas...

Day 205 — Archangel Raziel

"You are well supported. You don't have to hold all the balls in the air. Call upon me to help you bring fun into the equation again. It is only the mind that makes things complex. At the source of creation, there is simplicity and playfulness. Your heart knows this. Be at peace as you dance with your creations with lightheartedness. The youth of your soul is always within to brighten things up through play."

Notes, inspired writing or other brainstorming ideas...

Day 206 — Archangel Michael

"When inspiration arrives at your doorstep holding a bouquet of flowers know we have been working our blessings into the fabric of your daily world. You haven't missed a beat. You cannot get it wrong. When you dive into the fabric from right where you are, in the eternal now, do you realize the rest of the intricate fabric of your life is being woven for you in synchronized fashion by teams of Angels? Rest assured by beginning anew in this now moment, miracles are being sewn that will openheartedly greet you with humbled awareness."

Notes, inspired writing or other brainstorming ideas...

Day 207 – Archangel Raphael

"No time is better than now to expect the best for yourself. With this new beginning, let all the old internal programming fall away and be transformed into your higher potential for your life and service to the world. The light of the Divine and all of us are expanding you at this time. This expansion may feel uncomfortable and scary at times but there is nothing lost, only more of your exquisite potential gained. Let this shifting happen deep inside your cells… for what comes after is the most beautiful colored rainbow you can imagine!"

Notes, inspired writing or other brainstorming ideas...

Day 208 – Archangel Michael

"We send you frequencies today for your family lineage DNA clearing. If you say yes, this will help heal your ancestry from the beginning of their time on earth. No one will be forgotten. This healing is important for the bloodline to transform issues at the DNA level and also to be carriers of the higher frequencies from us Mother Earth dearly needs. One person in the family receiving DNA healing has a ripple effect, trickling down to all."

Notes, inspired writing or other brainstorming ideas...

Day 209 – Archangel Haniel

"Your love is your greatest power. We are honoring you today. For you remembering how much love you have inside of you creates a ripple effect of love into the entire cosmos. You feeling loved and cherished in whatever way that inspires you sends out harmonic creation vibes so purely that others seeking this in harmony tone are magnetically drawn in to bathe in the love light circles created. We dance with you today in sonic vibrations of love connection. Cheers to you being the real you."

Notes, inspired writing or other brainstorming ideas...

Day 210 – Archangel Michael

"There is so much love surrounding you. You are loved and shown the way every day with what feels pure, joyful and uplifting to your heart and soul. There is a reason for every encounter. Trust that you did make a difference. Some meetings between souls happen so that the love and trust within self is strengthened. For without meeting those that present you with a trial, you would not have the same opportunity to grow in areas that still need fortifying. The bud must break through the dirt in order to become a flower in full bloom."

Notes, inspired writing or other brainstorming ideas...

Day 211 – Archangel Ariel

"We are smiling with you today. We see you have walked through some veils that were holding you back for a time. Now the progress can be steady and much fun. We are revealing to you the stepping stones along your path. Trust the ones that feel good, skipping the stones that feel like sinkers… dancing in Divine Joy all the way. We are holding up a toast of complete and utter respect, love, support and sweetness for you. You have already arrived."

Notes, inspired writing or other brainstorming ideas...

Day 212 — Archangel Michael

"The time has come for everyone on the planet to have the opportunity to shift out of the old constrictions and thought forms. When you hit a brick wall and cannot figure something out is when the most viable solutions are waiting for you just past the brick and mortar. You could use your own might to get through the bricks or you may consider a very simple solution of asking me specifically for the highest and best solution available that will uplift all involved. Usually we already have it waiting, but unless you ask, The Archangels cannot intervene. We want to make this so easy for you. Solutions are there for anything you are facing. Ask and ye shall receive. It may surprise you how fast the resolution arrives."

Notes, inspired writing or other brainstorming ideas...

Day 213 – Archangel Gabriel

"Your life is one of unique perspective. You have teams of angels working behind the scenes for you, setting things into motion. When you focus upon what you'd prefer, we help bring you more of that. It's delightful to watch things unfold for you. Hold true to what you know you want and watch the miracles unfold before you."

Notes, inspired writing or other brainstorming ideas...

Day 214 – Archangel Michael

"When you ask me to surround your car with my light of protection I do so with heartfelt honor. When you ask me to protect you on your walks, did you know I call in my warrior Angels to surround you and the area with Divine Protection? You are never alone, my sweet and dear friend. What you treasure, we also hold near and dear to us. All that is grace, love, peace and joy is what you came here to bring the earth and her people. Through your light shining all the way to heaven's door we too can shine our light through you. The stars wink at you at night as you allow more joy, bliss and peace into your heart. Be at peace today knowing we support you and bring more goodness for you that's here to stay."

Notes, inspired writing or other brainstorming ideas...

Day 215 — Archangel Daniel

"Have faith our child, what seems okay or merely good now is about to get a whole lot better with time like a fine wine. Drink the good times in. Soak up the Mother Nature joy raptures. Sing with the hummingbirds. Bliss out with the sunsets. How good are you willing to let it get. We bring in healing tones for your heart today to expand your heartsong choirs of love. You deserve this. I am the Archangel that heals your heart for love. When you get the next moment to lay on Mother Earth, call Archangel Michael and myself in to send you these heart healing tones while you are laying on your back gazing at the floating clouds. These healing tones will be made specifically for you for where your heart-song is headed in its love landscape journey here upon the earth. Your heart tones will then magnetically attract into your life all that is good and all that is Divinely blessed for your life. We love all of you. Even those parts of yourself you hide away in a box. Allow those parts of self to merge and become one with your heart-song today, for they too deserve love's Divine Embrace."

Notes, inspired writing or other brainstorming ideas...

Day 216 – Archangel Michael

"Celebration abounds for you. What once was arduous is being made easy. Remember to continue to ask your body what it needs as you take pauses in your day. What will help you most now is staying in tune to the rhythms of your body. What unfolds from here are rainbows of sweet times and waterfalls of refreshment."

Notes, inspired writing or other brainstorming ideas...

Day 217 – Archangel Raphael

"Trust yourself. What was once good for you may not be right now. Wisdom comes from moment by moment listening, tuning in, asking for our assistance anytime you need us. Through quieting the mind we are able to bring you healing frequencies that calm your body systems, mind and heart. Allow these healing frequencies to permeate all of your being today. Take a breather. Feel your own heart beat. Take a break. Be okay with what is, just for a time. All is going to be okay. We are with you. You are well."

Notes, inspired writing or other brainstorming ideas...

Day 218 – Archangel Michael

"Cosmic connections are happening at lightning speed. These types of connections are needed to assist the planetary ascension with her evolution into a higher state of being. The darkness cannot stay as these cosmic connection points of light meet here in the physical in order to light a blaze ahead of them so others may have a well lit path to follow. We cannot state enough how important it is for you to let your light shine as bright as possible. No one benefits from the dimming of your light. Once you light your cosmic flame, no one or nothing can put it out. The cosmic part of you knows this because it can never die. Your light will always only shine brighter, for there can be no other way."

Notes, inspired writing or other brainstorming ideas...

Day 219 – Archangel Metatron

"There once was a time when all was one. Humanity is in dire straits craving to be at the center point of oneness again. One with all living creatures. One with God. One with Divine Mother. One with the ever expanding Universe. One with joy. One with love. Sometimes substitutes are formed to replace what the soul is really craving. What one craves usually is a substitute for the real thing. What's under the hood of the initial craving is usually a way to temporarily fill the void of the pain or emptiness feelings. To satiate your soul, you must call upon a desire to be fulfilled beyond the physical. This desire being oneness with Source Energy from which you came. Some call this God, The Divine or Oneness. We also call this home. There is nothing else that can fill the voided spaces like home light can, that from which you came. Let your heart receive this light of love from us today. Let there be no plans for tomorrow or the next day. Let now be the only thing that matters to your heart. Your heart wants to be free from that which drags it down. It is time, Yes? Allow the wings of all the Archangels including our dearly beloved Archangel Michael to take you there in this most fabulous moment of your time. Allow your enlightenment to happen in this no time cocoon with all of the Archangels. What once was, no longer exists. Let what is happening now, be the only thing that is alive within you, in this no time space place of existence from within your sacred heart. Breathe this in and know… everything that is good will remain. And so it is."

Notes, inspired writing or other brainstorming ideas . . .

Day 220 – Archangel Michael

"Long ago there was a cherished time on earth where no destruction occurred. This seems short lived in the entire scheme of things with the massive evolution our beloved Mother Earth has gone through. It has been a long journey indeed our friends, a very long tiresome adventure for many earth helpers. Many feel in dire straits and distraught at this time on earth. We ask our beloved friends to not lose all hope, for the time is nearing of a rebirth of this planet of an easier way for many. Let your path be lit by all of the Archangels and Ascended Masters light. Our purpose is to shine a light upon you and raise you up. You are very wise souls incarnated here in this time and place with Mother Earth to help her and all of humanity ascend into The Golden Era, The Enlightened Time of Being upon the planet once again. Rest assured the trials of the soul can be won. Ask for our assistance with all internal battles. Allow me to pick up your sword so you can finally rest for a while. I will keep you safe in the deep of the night so that our Father and Mother's Light will transcend any suffering into golden blessings upon your life."

Notes, inspired writing or other brainstorming ideas...

Day 221 – Archangel Raphael

"The love of you runs deep. You are learning to say, "No, thank you" to what feels like entrapment and "Yes, more please" to what gives your heart flight like an eagle soaring. The burdens of the heart from long ago are being lifted for you now. Breathe in the knowingness that yesteryear does not need to repeat itself. You are on the right railroad track for you now. We rock you to sleep tonight in the Divine's sweet embrace. You are well on your way and your soul is very proud."

Notes, inspired writing or other brainstorming ideas...

Day 222 – Archangel Michael

"Forgive yourself for standing in your truth. This lifetime is about that for you. The anger and regret you've once felt does not need to be held onto any longer. You know enough now to proceed differently. All of the Archangels and God are giving you strength today and for the rest of your life for you to stand in your power. It is no longer needed or advised on earth to give away one's power for the sake of receiving love, for you already have the love from heaven's door. The gates of love will always be unlocked for you. Breathe eternal love in, we assure you it is here to stay."

Notes, inspired writing or other brainstorming ideas...

Day 223 – Archangel Ariel

"Joy begets more joy and is contagious like a good belly laugh. What expands you with pure joy is readily available through you calling it in. Often when struggle or pain is at hand it is even more important to remember that joy is just around the bend from pain. We'd like you to strengthen your joy muscles more. One of the easiest ways is through laughing with a friend or conversing about what inspires you both. Another way is by playing in nature and listening to what the trees have to say to you. Allow joy fires of sweet happiness to spread through your days, weeks and months. See how quickly you can leap into the joy arena by asking yourself what is it that would really bring me nourishing, heart sustaining joy today? We meet you there on your longevity joy hill, just around the bend with white rose petals upon your feet."

Notes, inspired writing or other brainstorming ideas...

Day 224 — Archangel Michael

"It is not your job to carry others. They must do the work themselves. When you have done all you have been asked to do for your part and are not led to higher pastures, go forth, you have grace at your back. The feeling of needing to be responsible for another's good fortune is not yours to take on, it is theirs. There is a momentum that each individual has going for them or sometimes against them depending on other factors such as karma in this lifetime or other times and places. When you feel that momentum of karma of negative circumstances happening for someone else, to try to impede that, would most often take away the most valuable lessons their soul wants them to learn this time around. It may be alluring sometimes to assist them with taking the easy way out. But is that their soul is calling them toward for the most profound path of wisdom they signed up for? Could refusing a lifeline be actually giving one? You'll know the cutoff point(s) by the emotions you feel. If you feel your emotions rising to the brim out of frustration, anger, sadness, despair or feeling utterly depleted you'll know it may be time to draw the line in the sand. Some souls are not ready for the journey that beckons you forth. Their unpreparedness is a signal for you to spread your wings and trust the solo-flight."

Notes, inspired writing or other brainstorming ideas...

Day 225 – Archangel Raphael

"When a family member or friend is not feeling well, their energy doesn't feel as vibrant as it usually does, or they are ill, call me in to send them a continuous stream of healing light through God's light. What brings the most healing of all sometimes is through prayer and for the good wishes for all. When your mind is feeling troubled, those close to you can feel this too. Ask us to clear and heal all worried thoughts from your body, mind and soul on all levels. The peace we bring you holds the light coded seeds of love in them that can heal anything that ails them. One person in complete peace creates a wave pattern of healing for all who know you and for the entire vicinity in which you reside."

Notes, inspired writing or other brainstorming ideas...

Day 226 - Archangel Michael

"It's not the falling down that matters. Will you choose to love yourself again and again, for this is what counts. Blaming yourself for others burdens, guilt or misguided truths only serves to downplay the integrity of what you have come to realize. Speaking your truth from your heart allows everyone involved to reach higher mountains and greener pastures. What has been the God's honest words spoken from your heart through love, holds within it seeds of awareness that other people may choose to allow to blossom at some point in their lives. When these seeds are ready to be born into spring flowers within them, they will germinate and grow. Now it's God's time to water the seeds for them through the journey of their soul's evolution on earth. You have done enough our dear friend. Hand this situation to God now in a beam of golden light and allow the burdens to be lifted from you completely. The pathway will be lit up for them in doing so. May you know how much your contribution has indeed made a difference."

Notes, inspired writing or other brainstorming ideas...

Day 227 – Archangel Ariel

"Some come and go and some stay in your life for the rest of your days here. Where there is true blue friendship there is Divine Love at its best. Some bonds are unbreakable. They may tether a bit for a while, but new threads of love are sewn. When a friendship stays like this, know it is a gift of the highest accord. Heart-songs of love are played for an eternity; two heart bonds are meant to find each other through Divine Will in order. The form of the friendship may change, but the sweet love song remains. This was a chosen one, believe this to be true. You were meant to meet to shine even brighter like the stars that you both are."

Notes, inspired writing or other brainstorming ideas...

Day 228 — Archangel Michael

"When one tries too hard, sometimes the point is missed. If you knew you were completely taken care of what would you do? Asking yourself this each morning will help you avoid having regrets of any kind. What elevates your life is remembering how taken care of you are. The sun rises and sets without you trying to do anything to "make" that happen. Allow yourself to be carried by the current of support, love and gentleness that is here for you. Your heart need not be fixated on any end result or uphill battle any longer. Picture yourself at the top of the hill. All that is love is supporting you. What are you guided to do in the flow of gentleness and ease with all the love that is backing you?"

Notes, inspired writing or other brainstorming ideas...

Day 229 – Archangel Metatron

"To know you is to love you. Do not feel pressured by others who feel they know best for you or who want to guide you to what would work best for them. This is your life and you have the freedom to choose. Your earth journey is a unique one and is not written in stone. Others may sing the blues around you, but it doesn't mean you have to join them in the camaraderie of their misery to help pull them back up. This is where we come in. Asking us to bless your beloveds brings christened rose petals at their feet that feed them with light beams of encoded love, support, renewed health, peace, and joy. One prayer holds this power within it. For it is in your asking that the entire earth shall receive her bounty. So too shall you receive your glory through your sincerity of heart. Let the riches of your soul come forth into the world and be blessed by us, so that the many may be flooded with the Creator's love for them through the love we hold for you that you have released like a million newly winged butterflies just hatched from their cocoon."

Notes, inspired writing or other brainstorming ideas...

Day 230 — Archangel Michael

"Sometimes the sadness that passes through is not yours to carry. Sometimes the sadness is a sign that higher learning is involved between souls who have known each other before. Allow the wisdom on the higher planes to be brought unto you that hold the wisdom of the ages. We can do this for you if you ask. You do not have to carry burdens from other's choices. Surrender these burdens to us and allow us to communicate with those who have hurt you in anyway. This helps them and you release long standing grief that could be surfacing from many, many lifetimes ago that's ready for release. In asking for our help with those who you may hold sadness about, your heart will be freed, lifted up and anointed with the purest of love again."

Notes, inspired writing or other brainstorming ideas...

Day 231 — Archangel Ariel

"Be willing to see this situation or circumstance as we do. All souls involved are mending. What weighs heavy upon you is in transformation mode. You do not need to heal any of the others. The one that needs our attention now is you. Forgive yourself, for you have done nothing wrong. You are a mender, a fixer and the one to mend is deep forgiveness of yourself for allowing yourself to love at the depth that you do. There is nothing to forgive here, you see? Only to let yourself off the hook. All others around you must do their own work, their own processes of self discovery and excavation. In doing so they will be lifted up by us also. You are the one to pay attention to now. We love you and want you to not punish yourself for any love you have given. For it was genuine love that was cherished. Turning this love back onto yourself is not selfish, it is self forgiveness. Savoring the timeless moments with you is what's in order now. We are with you holding your hand."

Notes, inspired writing or other brainstorming ideas...

Day 232 – Archangel Michael

"Allow the love in your heart to permeate all of your being-ness today, knowing all is being taken care of. We want you to enjoy this moment, right here, right now. You deserve to be free of all heavy burdens your heart once held. Let the joy frequencies we send you today set your heart free and ground you with happiness currents of love."

Notes, inspired writing or other brainstorming ideas...

Day 233 — Archangel Raphael

"Place anything that troubles you into the palm of my hands right now and ask me to bless this area of your life and heal it. What brings you peace, healing, longevity, joy and all that is good will be delivered unto you in return. Allow yourself to receive my healing light I send to you right now, through your crown chakra. You are a child of the highest light of God and the love He has for you has never been forsaken. There is a flame of light that is held for you inside God's heart. This can never be put out and never dies. Ask that you return to your Divine Creator's heart each night before you sleep and I will meet you there to continue healing anything that ails you."

Notes, inspired writing or other brainstorming ideas...

Day 234 – Archangel Michael

"Your Soul's Mission upon this earth is directly tied to your greatest strength. What good results have you seen in your own life that you may have shared with others? What comes almost effortlessly for you? Sometimes if you have tried to put your Soul's Calling out into the world and doors are not opening like you expected it may be that you bringing your gifts into the world could be more fun than you are making it to be. What issues are facing the ideal people you'd like to work with? Speaking and sharing about what society is experiencing today helps you build rapport with your audience. You may also ask us to show you who you are to reach out to with your Life Purpose; what types of people. This begins the journey with discovering many more doors that will open through God's Grace and blessings that are always shining ever so brightly upon your life and Soul's Calling."

Notes, inspired writing or other brainstorming ideas...

Day 235 – Archangel Gabriel

"The earth is in her process of energetic renewal right now. With this comes many who are feeling out of sorts because of all the shifting of energy on earth so Mother Earth can transform her etheric body into a higher state of light. Higher light codes are being given to Mother Earth so that she can ascend into the Golden Era on Earth, Heaven on Earth. She needs your assistance at this time… the more you ask for higher light, the most brilliant Divine light that you can call in from God brings Mother Earth more light, thus helping her release all that is stifling to her as well. As this process continues it is ever so important to take care of yourself by grounding your energy into Mother Earth daily and spending time with her in prayer. Thinking about the better life you are creating for yourself ushers in positive vibrations for her and all of the Earth's creatures. What can you do during the next 24 hours that will help you feel as peaceful as a lion cub with her nurturing mama? We send you peace-waves of healing today so any worry you have felt is bathed in waterfalls of Divine Mother's love for you."

Notes, inspired writing or other brainstorming ideas...

Day 236 – Archangel Michael

"The sleep that you need depends little upon the hours that you have worked and more upon the vital life force energy you currently have in your body systems to sustain you, as well as the living life force nutrients you intake daily with your food. Spending quality time with your feet upon the earth barefoot also draws in light from the etheric realms and from the sun that revitalize you from the zero point energy force. Breathing fresh ions in the air daily, as deep as possible to the base of your lungs assists all of your brain cells to renew themselves by the minute. The light of creation breathes and recreates again and again. So too can you as you age, create renewed sustainable energy for yourself that births love creations into the world. Allow the Divine Flow, some call this the Holy Flow to breathe new life into all of your cells daily, through your vibrant food choices and through your time with exquisite Mother Nature. The next chance you get, ask Mother Nature to recharge you with her sustaining pulse of light as you stand upon her with your bare feet, or lie down upon her back. Breakthrough moments happen as you make a practice of this. Call us in to meet you there and ask for a breakthrough with any stuck situations you are facing and you'll feel the dawn of a magical new day breaking at sunrise."

Notes, inspired writing or other brainstorming ideas...

Day 237 – Archangel Ariel

"Getting things done happens at a higher frequency when you rest up to build up your energy and complete tasks when the energy is there to do so. If your energy is lagging for the given list of items you need to get done, ask yourself if more time in nature is needed to refuel or if better quality nutrition may be necessary to allow deeper healing inside all of your tissues to occur. Refueling can come in many various forms. After you have rebuilt your energy reserves and asked us to clear your mind, body and soul from any inhibiting thoughts, energies or resistances that may be getting in the way of you taking inspired action, look for those ever so slight openings of creative energy to enter into the wave of. Those creative surges will expand when you take action when the flow moments begin. Watch the flow, call us in, listen for the quest, experiment and see what happens. Staying in a continuous state of flow can be felt when you listen closely to the sacred wisdom of your body. What does your body need? What is it telling you today? What does it need from you? Listen closely and follow its lead, not forcing it to go very far beyond its energy level limits restores equilibrium to your body, mind and soul as other healthy practices are enjoyed."

Notes, inspired writing or other brainstorming ideas...

Day 238 — Archangel Michael

"You are an integral part of the fiber of humanity and the earth's evolutionary process. You make a difference every time you treat yourself with the utmost respect, love and tenderness. It is through this self-honoring that abundance flows. You are enough, you are more than enough. Your worthiness has never been in question by us. The value of you is not based on other's opinions of you…you are of value because you come from the Divine Creator, you are Divine by nature. That said…it is time for you to be that which you already are. You are Divine. You are enough. You are worthy. You deserve Love in all its forms."

Notes, inspired writing or other brainstorming ideas...

Day 239 – Archangel Raphael

"There is no need for you to suffer any longer. Joy is here for you in a substantial way. No amount of you suffering will ease the suffering of others. You healing yourself and asking us to help is what lifts the pain for others. You lead by example. Your joy gives others permission to allow theirs in too. Be like the hummingbirds singing and chirping in the shade trees. Feed off that which brings your heart the utmost sustaining happiness. You deserve this kind of good lovin'. We are smiling for the bright shining light that you are. All is uplifted in the presence of the Divine You."

Notes, inspired writing or other brainstorming ideas...

Day 240 — Archangel Michael

"Whatever brings you the most ease of being and lifts you up higher helps pave the way for many. The steps you are guided to take may not feel comfortable at first, but as you listen to the daily inspired actions we are encouraging you to make, your joy levels will increase significantly. There is nothing more delightful than watching you grow, blossom and expand into who we know you to already be. You are held in a protection of Christ Light as you become the more of you that is waiting to greet you with open arms."

Notes, inspired writing or other brainstorming ideas...

Day 241 — Archangel Ariel

"Speaking your truth from your heart with love helps loosen the noose of silence. What can prevent one from speaking their truth could be imprints of betrayal, abuse or abandonment in their cellular memory bank. The strongholds from lifetimes of silence can sometimes bleed into this lifetime and affect the body's health and the feelings of freedom to speak one's truth. Ask us to energetically loosen any silencing shackles you may have and lift them up and out of your entire body, mind and soul. We will also transform any imprints from the past that may be holding you back from speaking your full truth. As you free yourself, others too can become freed by your example. There is no better time than now to allow us to assist you like this. Connecting you to your Divine Source of Light is our greatest honor."

Notes, inspired writing or other brainstorming ideas...

Day 242 — Archangel Michael

"The veil is thinning between dimensions and other worlds of existence. Those who have passed can hear you. Every thought you have about them reaches them. Even friends here in the physical can now hear each other's thoughts more readily. What you speak, say or think can either hurt or heal others. We are here to help you put your feelings into words that heal. This not only uplifts you, but the entire planet. Uplifting yourself with loving thoughts about yourself is where it starts. When you are kind towards self when you rewind, you heal your past."

Notes, inspired writing or other brainstorming ideas...

Day 243 — Archangel Evangeline

"As you let go of outside perceptions, which are based on that person's limited perspective (inside their world), you open yourself up to the real gifts of heaven. The door is wide open for your soul's gifts to flourish, expand and cultivate as you blossom beyond what other think, feel, say or do. Call upon me to sprinkle you with abundant blessings from your true source. You'll know I'm near when you feel a smile on your face and sometimes there are flashes of uplifting light appearing on your walls or in your peripheral view. You deserve the blessings I share with you from the Divine."

Notes, inspired writing or other brainstorming ideas...

Day 244 — Archangel Michael

"Celebrate the moment. This moment right now is enough. You are cocooned in a circle of light today for comfort, love, support and heart nourishment. Take the pressure off yourself to be anything for anyone else right now and just allow yourself to be enough for you. This is all that you need to do; be okay with you right here, right now. All you have ever longed for is unfolding in Divine timing that is right for you. All the eternal goodness is here for you…enveloping you and loving you all the way home. For you are enough. You always have been more than enough. Grace is with you."

Notes, inspired writing or other brainstorming ideas…

Day 245 – Archangel Gabriel

"Now is a time on earth where the battle can be won through peaceful healing and lovingly speaking your truth with appropriate boundaries in place. The darkness falls away with the light of love. Darkness has no power when bathed in Divine Love. Warriors can still carry their swords, however what's needed most in the world at this time is more love and tenderness towards those who know not what they do. Forgiveness and peace calm the waters of the heart. Love's well is never ending and lifts souls from the depths of despair more graciously than a sword ready for battle. The sword may always be near your side, but allow your heart's natural power of love to expand and connect to those in your presence so their Divine Soul Treasures may be found."

Notes, inspired writing or other brainstorming ideas...

Day 246 – Archangel Michael

"What lesson in your life do you feel you keep repeating? Any moment you feel you are walking into the abyss with the same ole', same ole pattern, call upon me to bring in the flow of what may work better. The repeating of what is familiar happens for many, lifetime after lifetime. This is your time to allow us to help you break free of the chains that have bound you up. That which has seemed impossible to break free from now is made possible this time around. Name what you'd like our assistance with today and allow things to be easier upon you. Place the pattern or area of concern into a ball of white light and hand it to me. I now take this ball of white light with your area of concern and assist you at the soul level with the transformation you have been waiting eons of time for. What once was seemingly impossible, is indeed made possible. You are free my friend, you are freed from the outworn limitations of times long past."

Notes, inspired writing or other brainstorming ideas...

Day 247 – Archangel Metatron

"Call upon me to assist you with building abundance creation skills. This is also what I help my students with on the inner planes. What helps you live in the waterfalls of the abundance which is always waiting for you is learning how your skill-sets meet humanity's needs. Can you be free and prosperous at the same time? This is in fact available for you as you are willing to go beyond your comfort zone into new ideas and concepts about where money comes from. The income that is yours could quadruple this year if you were to allow in higher concepts of how you can use your Divine Gifts to assist in raising humanity to its next level of awareness. The ideas of selling your soul, your time, your innermost ethical standards in exchange for the dollar is crumbling before your eyes. These old concepts of how money is to be "earned" in exchange for monetary reward is shifting into the ability to manifest what you need with not only your thoughts, but your vast ideas we are bringing to you. For more abundance is everywhere and can indeed manifest for you in a multitude of ways. What makes people miss how their gifts can bring opportunities to many is their thoughts about how money arrives for them. It is time to allow your previous training of any "working for the dollar" to enter into a new era of pure prosperity through sharing your joy with the world. Allowing in concepts of Divine Money, God's Money, Money through Divine Will feels far out there for many, yet it is where the most abundance is allocated with freedom attached to its tail. Exchange the word God for the Divine or the Creator if that is how you identify better here. When you ride on the shirt tales of your Divine Expression through the highest divine order for your life by surrendering how you thought it should go and asking for God's Will be done, you allow for the most abundance imaginable to enter your world. For this is the world you are co-creating here, is it not? What brings forth your knowledge of how this works? Simply ask. For this is my specialty and I bring you sacred geometry light codes today for abundant living upon the planet. You saying Yes assists all others to see the example you live by and be able to do the same. You are a leader, our friend. Go forth and claim what has always been your birthright of Divine Abundance to live through you. The way is being made for you. Believe this and so shall it be."

Day 248 – Archangel Michael

"What helps you forgive is to know that the children have been lost for quite some time. They have been misled and misguided. The anger falls away with the realization that nothing is personal. All that has happened is in Divine Order. What was meant to happen has. Allow your heart to be free of all the guilt it holds. Thinking you are helping the other by hanging onto these emotions serves no one. Your recognition and realization of the illusion has already helped free them. Only love remains."

Notes, inspired writing or other brainstorming ideas...

Day 249 — Archangel Metatron

"There once was a time when those on earth needed to stay together for survival. Some still choose this alignment as a couple. When your consciousness has been elevated to be able to see, feel and sense many quantum realities at once, survival becomes a matter of choice rather than circumstance. What limits those that cannot see or sense multi platinum options here is their connection to the Creator, which is where their true power source is never ending, always beginning and never runs out of options, ideas, resources, time and income. When one forsakes the journey of their soul for a physical scarcity role model they have forgotten the bigger picture completely. Where is the missing link? It is not within lacking resources or a misguided connection of where those resources actually come from. The empowered soul realizes their resources come from harmonious alignment to all that is and all that ever was. You see, the Creator's Love for you is never ending and ever beginning, it always was and will be. Once this is tapped into for good, the scarcity of resources mindset disappears. We align you today and harmonize your energy system with Creation, with God, with the Divine. All the shackles are falling away now and you are remembering the truth of your infinite supply."

Notes, inspired writing or other brainstorming ideas...

Day 250 — Archangel Michael

"In your Divine Blueprint is your song. This song plays within your heart each and every day. Your song is as light and magical as a butterfly that dances its effervescent sweetness on a lovers sunset path. Will you stop and hear your song today?"

Notes, inspired writing or other brainstorming ideas...

Day 251 — Archangel Raphael

"Your perspective counts. You came into this world wanting to make a difference and you have. You have learned many things on your earth journey, some of which have not been easy, to say the least. Your courage carries seeds within it to help the generations after you. They will remember the day you chose life instead of leaving. You have given them the gift of choosing to birth new ideas, instead of going with the family lineage patterning and outdated programming. What will help generations to come is happening through you right now. We applaud your ability to endure when things looked grim. Cheers to a much brighter future ahead. You are worth living for."

Notes, inspired writing or other brainstorming ideas...

Day 252 – Archangel Michael

"Addiction has hit many families like a plague in the night. Addiction can also begin from wanting to "buck the system" and overturn the structures on earth that have been in place for so long and have not worked. When a dependency has a hold of a sensitive soul it can be a way to numb out the pain from many deeply held traumas. Archangel Raphael and myself assist in freeing those ready to be released from any strongholds. Place any dependencies you may have or someone close to you has inside a white and golden ball of light right now. Hand this ball of white and golden light to us and ask that those who are suffering from dependencies be healed and freed completely. We will do our part to lift those you prayer about from this very restrictive frequency and unbind them. May you know how much your prayers are heard. Without you praying for yourself and others we cannot intervene. Our greatest honor is to have the requests made so we can assist all who are suffering."

Notes, inspired writing or other brainstorming ideas...

Day 253 — Archangel Gabriel

"When someone gives you an opinion about your life that doesn't quite sit right or feels hurtful know they are coming from a place of hurt themselves. Often times they are crying out for love in ways that they don't even realize. The hurt that is coming out sideways from them usually is a defense mechanism to try and protect that which they feel extremely vulnerable about. Picture a person that comes to mind here and place them in a ball of golden light and hand them to me asking their heart be mended and healed completely on all levels of their being. Much healing, releasing and tender Angelic love will happen for all involved now. This hurtful situation has been divinely blessed. What will bring a smile to your face the rest of the day? Be in the love of that and know miracles are at play."

Notes, inspired writing or other brainstorming ideas...

Day 254 – Archangel Michael

"When you have drawn a line in the sand and communicated your preferences to someone and you have not been honored, know that this situation came about to assist in the healing for all involved. What once brought pleasure, yet no longer does, is showing you that there is some deep releasing needed of what does not serve you and your higher purpose. To release the rest of what happened, you may place that person, circumstance or event into a white globe of light and hand it to me. Ask that all involved be freed from old strongholds on your souls, all the outworn pain from long ago and any anguish or regret residue that remains be transformed back into love. You may close your eyes and do this now if you'd like. We are assisting all involved on the higher planes of consciousness with healing all the core issues involved here. From this point forward allow yourself to focus upon what feels best for you to spend your attention, your energy and your time upon. You just performed the ultimate healing quest for this situation. All is in Divine Order. May peace prevail and be with you now and forevermore."

Notes, inspired writing or other brainstorming ideas...

Day 255 – Archangel Ariel

"Let your mind be free of troubles that may come to be tomorrow. Spend your focus upon the simple tasks that can be completed today and don't leave out the joy of pondering moments in nature. What your soul desires for you is freedom from the worries of tomorrow. Asking daily that your Will be aligned to the Will of the Divine (or God) creates the worries of tomorrow to work out for the highest and best good of all involved. Did you know this?… What tomorrow may bring may alter 11 times over depending upon many factors of other people's decision making process. This is why we urge you to pray for those around you that they may receive healing from us on all levels of their being. As you do this the outcomes of the future are ascended to blessed circumstances for all. Every single one of your prayers are heard. Please never doubt this. We need your prayers for those who are suffering. This brings light to them which may otherwise could not reach them. Your prayers give us permission to assist. Be free from worry, our dear child. Worry steals your joy-now-moments in time. Allow Divine Will to orchestrate your future with many blessings that inspire the world at large."

Notes, inspired writing or other brainstorming ideas. . .

Day 256 – Archangel Michael

"When fear arises call me in. Christ and I work as a team together often. Terror frequencies and thought forms are prevalent on earth. When you were little you often felt not enough protection from the things that terrified you. We want you to know how protected you are as you call upon Christ and myself for the light of protection that is always available for you. We surround you today with the utmost protection like from Christ and myself, all the way up through the center of the Divine column of light and down into the center of Mother Earth's belly. If you should say yes, you would like this to be done for you, so shall it be. This healing and protection will begin the moment you say yes, all through the night until it is complete. What used to terrify you, need not be a concern any longer. Place what you fear into a ball of golden light and hand it to me now. Surrendering the need to control the outcome of this and allowing more protection light for yourself, connects you into the column of protected connection light that is always sustaining and delivers unto you never ending support. Allowing us to deliver you this gift brings more peace to our precious Mother Earth. She thanks you for this and so do we. May you feel honored, loved, respected and protected the rest of your Divine Days you walk upon this earth."

Notes, inspired writing or other brainstorming ideas...

Day 257 – Archangel Gabriel

"Closure begins with self forgiveness. Know you did nothing wrong here. You followed your inner promptings. Sometimes the path will lead you in one direction for only a very short amount of time before you come to a fork in the road. You chose the route that was most lit up for you. Forgive any others for not understanding the road you were called to. Forgive yourself for letting go and not holding on tightly enough. What others want from you no longer needs to shackle you. You chose correctly. The wisest road called you forth and you are now embarking upon a journey of the highest order. We commend you for this and are guiding each and every footstep. Your freedom beckoned you forth and the light of dawn continues to call you."

Notes, inspired writing or other brainstorming ideas...

Day 258 – Archangel Michael

"When you are ready for love's whisper it will be there. You have come too far not to allow love in when it arrives. There is power in surrendering the longing and allowing things to be as they are for now. What trips many up is the need to grab onto love's ride. You are beyond this now. When love's embrace houses sorrow for your soul you have learned to turn towards joy, peace and inner love. The love of your soul for you knows there is no more time for regrets. Peaceful days ahead call you forth into moonlit peace dance skies. Your lifeline does not belong in another's hands, only in your glorious Creator's heart. The heartbeat of love for you beats on and on and on… Always beginning again and again. The sorrowful days have transcended to life's love song for you. Cherish these glory days. You have learned a level of self mastery that called you forth into it through thick and thin. What comes next is better than good. The Divine herself has opened her doors to heaven on earth for you."

Notes, inspired writing or other brainstorming ideas...

Day 259 – Archangel Metatron

"Sometimes people show up in your life to show you that something you deemed once impossible IS possible. Your desire, as buried as it might be, has made it so. What caused that undeniable feeling of "knowing" was that your soul knew you were stepping onto a bridge. The bridge was unshakable and was only meant to be a short walk over to the other side. What was always waiting for you at the end of the bridge were glorious pastures of wildflowers and inter-dimensional sunsets. What you once wanted from long ago is complete and has altered. The ego always wants a sure thing, but once the ego surrenders to Divine Will it wants only what is for the greater good, you see? What once held you back no longer does because the ego is doing the Divine's dance."

Notes, inspired writing or other brainstorming ideas...

Day 260 — Archangel Michael

"Many of you are transitioning from the old 3D living, "old form ways", into a higher vibration of light living that some are terming the 5D (5th Dimensional) new world. This new world, the new earth sometimes goes even higher than the 5D vibration of light. The numbers do not matter so much as your willingness to trust there is a more substantial light form of thought being overlaid upon the earth at this time by us and the Ascended Masters in order to assist our dearly beloved Mother Earth and human evolution at this time raise to a more evolved, higher quadrant of light that is more life giving and sustaining to your body systems. Many are being asked to let go of the old way of doing things for a lighter way of being and living. Even the old 3D structures such as businesses and the way banks work are transcending to more of an etheric light structure through the air waves of the internet. If it feels like it is changing or crumbling in your life, it may just be your soul and your guides on the inner planes, the etheric levels that you also exist on, asking you to forgo the old way of doing things because a more substantial way of living, being and loving is available for you. Sometimes it is scary when change hits, but we assure you there are etheric light structures for your new life, your higher Divine Destiny that has already been built for you. Think of this as a bridge. Many etheric bridges are being built for those ready to be able to have a safe crossing to the higher dimensional ways of living that the earth is ascending to. Asking for your own transformational process to be easier for you. This helps us bridge you from the known 3D comfort zones of living into your ultimate Divine Destiny, Soul's Calling. As you take the initial higher states of being for yourself, you not only help yourself, but you are creating a bridge for others to feel safe enough to do the same. We commend you for your strength, your dedication and your unending love for humanity. Where there is love, there are higher dimensional light bridges being formed."

Day 261 — Archangel Ariel

"Pretending something isn't there doesn't make it go away. When you feel something is "off", it is. Others may ask you to look the other way so as to not make them uncomfortable. This is never advisable in our opinion. In doing so, their growth may be stunted. Standing your ground with what feels right for you will ultimately set your heart, body, mind and soul free. There is no need to buy into the sadness that you have hurt them by doing so. Carrying someone else's load of rocks for them may be a temporary solution, but not a permanent one. Call us in to support you both. As you move forward in the direction you are given by your higher team of guides and Angels you help the good of all. Close your eyes and feel into where you may be carrying someone else's burden. Picture a pink and golden sphere of light from me and place this burden into this light globe and hand it to me. Mother Mary and I will be assisting you with this on the etheric planes, the inner realms so that this heaviness is transformed into light, love and peace again. You are here as a transformer of the old suffering on earth. Be well in knowing you are supported by us and the Ascended Masters. We love you infinitely."

Notes, inspired writing or other brainstorming ideas...

Day 262 — Archangel Raphael

"Forgive yourself for leaping into the unknown. You are being recognized today for your bravery and your courage. This earth school is just short of insanity sometimes and we know this. To make sense of it sometimes feels undeniably crazy at times. The struggles you have gone through have been undeniably difficult. Many are being asked to wake up. In that waking up process there is a purging of the old systems out of each person's energy bodies. Some can make it through this process with more ease and grace than others. Many just tighten up and have energetic resistance to all the changes they are being asked to make. The support from us is unyielding; however, we know it can be a very bumpy ride at times. Many wake up out of their slumber and feel they are in a different dimensional world. They do not want to return to their bodies and some go lifetimes half in and half out of their bodies, not fully present with themselves and the world at large. This causes a disruption in the healthy functioning of their body systems. When one's consciousness is not fully present with self, the vital life force energy leaks out of one's body into the ethers, you see? This is why we are asking you at this time to be present with what you are sensing, feeling and being led to do in each moment so that you enter the flow. Not from a heady space, but a grounded sense of self flow. This is how we communicate with you best, when you are in a well grounded place. Spending more time in mother nature helps us communicate with you more effectively. Your guidance gets stronger each time you commune with nature. The next time you are in nature, call me in and ask me to bring you a sign that I am there. You'll surely receive one from me and it is my honor to greet you in this way."

Day 263 – Archangel Metatron

"Synchronicities are our way of knocking on the door of your awareness so you know where your flow is. When you are out of the flow, life may feel like a drudgery or you are forcing things into being. God's light flooding you creates the flow. How do you stay in the Divinely blessed flow of your life? Simply asking to be shown what your Highest Divine Path is for your life. What is your Divine Destiny? Asking to be shown this on a daily basis will bring the flow to you and cause the most miraculous synchronistic events, people and circumstances to show up at your doorstep unannounced. What seemed impossible will be made known to you through serendipitous happenings all around you. As you ask for your path to be aligned to your highest Divine Destiny, your Dharma, get ready for an incredibly magical ride. All that was a struggle before transforms into pure gold in your pathway."

Notes, inspired writing or other brainstorming ideas...

Day 264 – Archangel Gabriel

"When you first rise in the morning, placing your feet upon Mother Earth helps you begin your day in a connected way. The grounding love of Mother Earth connects your energy circuits to her healing powers. This also helps regulate your heartbeat and all of your organs. Too much time indoors causes the energetic flow through your body to jam up and not be as creative as you naturally are. A long walk in the mornings or afternoon opens up your Divine Creative Flow again. Breathe in fresh air as often as possible and you'll feel our love ever so present with you."

Notes, inspired writing or other brainstorming ideas...

Day 265 – Archangel Michael

"What the world needs most right now is love. Heart blazing love for all things, situations, people, critters and even haters. Where there is love there is least resistance. Energize love from your heart into all you are doing, all the activities of your day. Love dissolves pain. Love relinquishes fear. Love turns struggle into triumph. Where does love start? It begins with you. How do you wish you were loved more? Picture, feel and sense this now, feeling your heart expand into how you wish you were loved, in what ways? Place these longings into a golden sphere of light I hold for you now. Be open to receive how you want to be loved in different forms that feel good to you. Abundant rivers of love are flooding in now from the etheric realms where all of your Divine Treasures are stored."

Notes, inspired writing or other brainstorming ideas...

Day 266 – Archangel Raziel

"What has brought you to your knees in your life holds the power to bring awareness to many. Allow your freedom of speech to speak the words of truth your soul wants to communicate through you. Not holding this back for the sake of sounding weird or "too out there" helps free more souls than you may realize. Trying to "fit in" binds you up. Where in your life do you feel the constrictions of needing to fit into situations, groups or ideas about how you should be living to appease others? Whenever you find yourself needing to placate others for the sake of melding with the group or being welcomed you have come to a fork in the road. Ask us to assist you when at a crossroads. Ask us to show you what is for your Divine Life Purpose and what is not. Often times guilt feelings are not there to lift you higher, but are very old energies of not being rewarded when you didn't fit in or do what someone else wanted you to do. This is the time of the massive transformation of this guilt upon the planet. Let us free you today from any guilt you may hold about anything that has happened. Long held agreements from times past may need to be broken and ended. Let us lift you to your Himalayan freedom top. What frees you most definitely elevates others (even if not noticeable at first). The energetic elevation of souls is always interconnected. The time is ripe for you. Let Divine Will pave waves of grace into your evergreen paths."

Notes, inspired writing or other brainstorming ideas...

Day 267 – Archangel Michael

"Bringing closure to the past is welcomed. We support you in any areas of your life that you feel it is time to move on from. What once lifted you higher may have ended up creating a heavy burden for you. This is when you know it is time walk through a new door that offers you many more soul rich adventures that are waiting to expand you like a freedom dove in full flight. Give yourself permission to allow the outworn to simply fall away or hand them to us to unhook them and purify the energies there. What's waiting is love's embrace and soul-shine."

Notes, inspired writing or other brainstorming ideas...

Day 268 – Archangel Raphael

"Trust that which you already are. Be willing to make mistakes. Go forth and stand in your power. Stand tall and be you. You shine and stand out in a crowd of hundreds. It is your destiny to be great. Be willing to fumble sometimes. These times will teach you how to prevail through the muddiest of waters so you can teach it to others. The core fibers of you already are all that you wish to be. We are sending you light frequencies today to help you remember that which you are… divine by nature. Simply Divine you are!"

Notes, inspired writing or other brainstorming ideas...

Day 269 – Archangel Michael

"You are being reinvigorated today with a new freedom blueprint. If you say yes to receiving an upgraded emotional, mental, spiritual and physical freedom template, be ready for miraculous new beginnings to present themselves. Whenever you feel you are dragging yourself through mud or your thoughts feel heavy, please do ask us for upgraded Angelic blueprints. This way what will set you free on all levels becomes easily available to you in the form of ideas, your gifts enhanced, aha-moments and doors opening unexpectedly. All of the Angelic Kingdom has ladders available for you and humanity at this time. You are worth receiving a lift off into bluer skies and the sweet joy songs of hummingbird days. Ask and ye shall receive and it is so."

Notes, inspired writing or other brainstorming ideas...

Day 270 — Archangel Raphael

"There is no need for you to suffer any longer. Joy is here for you in a substantial way. No amount of your suffering will ease the suffering of others. You healing you and asking us to help is what lifts the pain for others. You lead by example. Your joy gives others permission to allow theirs in too. Be like the hummingbirds singing and chirping in the shade trees. Feed off that which brings your heart the utmost sustaining happiness. You deserve this kind of good lovin'. We are smiling for the bright shining light that you are. All is uplifted in the presence of the Divine You."

Notes, inspired writing or other brainstorming ideas...

Day 271 — Archangel Michael

"If guilt should happen after standing up for yourself with appropriate boundaries for yourself call upon me to untangle you and the other(s) energetically. The more you ask to be aligned to Divine Will the stronger you become and the less of a need there is to give in to the will of others for the sake of appeasing them. Close your eyes if you like and scan your body from head to toe. See where you may be carrying around the heaviness of guilt over something. Breathe deeply into this area and visually hand the heaviness over to me. I will be releasing you from this burden that you no longer need to carry in this lifetime and any others you are carrying. Sleep well tonight knowing this, for this is easy for me to do for you. Your heart will be restored to wholeness again the more you request this of me. It is my honor to lift you up and carry you beyond the struggle points into your dignified sunshine strength again."

Notes, inspired writing or other brainstorming ideas...

Day 272 – Archangel Raphael

"Humanity is at a crossroads right now. Many are recognizing the importance of simple living as a way of ease of being for their peace of mind and as a way of contributing to the planet by leaving a light footprint. What helps you have more peace of mind is what we are assisting you to follow right now. When making a buying decision ask yourself, in 5 – 10 years will this be more of burden to me or will this have added more peace to my life? We will help you see, sense and feel what items to purchase and which ones to pass on. Lightening your load of burdens is much needed right now. What lightens your heart, body, mind and soul is the way to go."

Notes, inspired writing or other brainstorming ideas...

Day 273 – Archangel Michael

"As annoyances arise during your day, call upon our dearly beloved friend Ganesha. He will sweep obstacles out of your pathway that seem to be never ending. When an annoyance keeps occurring again and again as you request energetic assistance from all of the Archangels and Ganesh you'll notice the irritation becoming more prevalent sometimes. This happens so that the problem is amplified enough to be able to see the components of it that are the root of the issue. Be thankful for the roots of these problems coming to the surface. It is a sure sign that the energetics of the situation or occurrence need more Divine light added to the equation. When you feel muffled from speaking your truth, call me in to remove the suppression energy in your system. Your good health depends upon the roots of these issues being healed and transformed. What is suppressed outside of you gets tangled up and can become a blockage to your chakra system. What annoyances in your life would you like our assistance with? Energetically place these into a beam - a column of sky blue light. Ganesh and I will be bringing in more support for you with this now. We bathe you with the calming waters of crystalline blue light now to calm your system from this inflammation. In releasing the need to control the outcome, we are able to uproot this issue permanently for you."

Notes, inspired writing or other brainstorming ideas...

Day 274 — Archangel Michael

"In this world many are feeling alone right now. We have our wings spread around those who call us in who are feeling blue. We shine God's brilliant light upon those that feel sad and who are weary from this most strenuous earth journey. The separation from God's light has felt like a rift in many souls, almost like a betrayal. We assure you that God has not forsaken or betrayed you or our Beloved Mother Earth. Mother Earth herself wept when the earth entered into darkness so long ago. You came here to be a light and safe space for many. The souls that grow the most are the ones that know that ultimately they have never been separate from God. Those that suffer the most have forgotten to call God's light in daily. Seek and ye shall find. Ask and it shall be given. When it feels like something is missing call us in to merge you into one with God's Light. The all encompassing love of all that is, embraces you now with the tenderness of her most beloved child. You are remembered and you have never been forgotten."

Notes, inspired writing or other brainstorming ideas...

Day 275 — Archangel Zadkiel

"The door that feels the most like freedom, love, tenderness and up-liftment is the door to continue walking through. When you are about to open a door and it feels restrictive, stifling or heavy, ask us to come in with you to guide you and show you whether this door is for you or not. If it is not we will guide you back out of this door into a brilliant hallway with more doors. You'll know the one to walk through when it bursts wide open for you with brilliant unrestricting light that breathes life into your wings. This is the door we are guiding you to now. All the love from your heart to know you are well on your way."

Notes, inspired writing or other brainstorming ideas...

Day 276 – Archangel Michael

"Where in your life do you need more balance? What areas of your life feel like you are spinning your wheels, no matter how hard you try to make things stay the same? When you are at your wits end, during these segments of your day you know it is time to surrender the self-effort. Find a spot to sit in nature and let go of forcing anything. This will bring your body systems back into a harmoniously peaceful flow. Where you once had to make things happen, we ask you to simply let go of trying too hard. Picture this area of your life that feels too forced and place it in the palms of my hands now and say, "May Thy will be done on earth as it is in heaven." Taking a deep breath and let it go. That's all that's needed at this present moment. That seed has been planted for the highest outcome to occur for the good of all."

Notes, inspired writing or other brainstorming ideas . . .

Day 277 — Archangel Gabriel

"Trust yourself with your Divine Gifts bestowed upon you from God. Your Divine Mother and Father want you to move forward with your inspired ideas and gifts you naturally have. When you feel the prompting, proceed. Please do not judge your precious work. Think of it as a baby God has given to you to take care of. Would you belittle that baby with your thoughts and words? That baby is God's gift to you to nurture, love and raise with tender loving care. Hold your creation, your idea close to your heart and rock it every day with encouraging thoughts and tender loving care. For every stroke of the brush is sent with heaven's grace. Let each stroke be from the heart through the love of doing each and every step and know that your work is blessed. You have permission and it is time."

Notes, inspired writing or other brainstorming ideas...

Day 278 – Archangel Michael

"You are a valued member of the community and society at large. Your light is like a lighthouse in the night for many souls trying to find their way home. Your job is not over yet, you have much more love to give. Shine your light upon even the desperate ones so they may know where God's love resides. When love is untainted and from the heart it gives a passageway for others to find their path. What helps one, helps all. There is no need to give until depletion, only to shine your light brighter upon all things that enter your path. We assure you, more troubled souls need your beacon of light to light the way for them in the dark of the night. In doing so, your life will be blessed with abundance miraculously for the rest of your days here."

Notes, inspired writing or other brainstorming ideas...

Day 279 – Archangel Chamuel

"Your greatness has not been lost by the wayside from this life's trials and tribulations. The disappointment you sometimes feel is to be expected with all that has taken place. We are working with you to erase any residues of self doubt. The old programming that humanity has is very repressive and has not allowed for many to rise above this old energetic structure of lack and doubt. Many have hidden as a way to self preserve. To free yourself from the outdated restrictions you know are not you happens with the asking of all that is not Divinely you to be transformed into what is truly you, your full soul's essence returned to you through God's Grace and love for you. As you do this, our Angelic healing teams will arrive and begin their beautiful light work to heal these aspects of self. Feeling like you haven't done enough is a falsity, for you have. Breathe this in now. You are enough. You are Divine Light in physical form. Let the limiting beliefs about any so called failures be transformed completely now in God's Grace. Let your heart continue to be strengthened by all that Love that is wrapping you with now."

Notes, inspired writing or other brainstorming ideas...

Day 280 – Archangel Michael

"What stings like a deep, fresh cut does not need to scar you. When you befriend the enemy in your mind and heart you befriend yourself wholeheartedly. What helps the little one within is remembering how to love yourself with the utmost care. Anxiety is a sign that there is more self nurturing to do with healing those aspects of self that have been abused or shunned to the side. When you are too hard on yourself these aspects of self that have been hurt in the past may sneak up on you and try to get your attention. If one self medicates in an attempt to quiet these inner voices these aspects of self will try new ways to get your attention. Sometimes accidents happen or mishaps in life happen because there are certain aspects of self that are crying out to be healed, loved and integrated into wholeness again with Divine Light, through God's light. One can break out of these old patterns with clearer thinking, but if the aspects of self that have been split off have not been integrated into wholeness again by being sent back to high self for healing, more mishaps or physical events in the 3D world may keep happening to get your attention, it means that more of an integration of self is needed. Call me in when mishaps or painful events happen and ask me to integrate all aspects of self that have been fragmented in all timelines, past, present and future and integrate them into wholeness again. Ask me to cut all cordings between anyone else involved. In doing so I will be assisting you with completing your healing process here on earth so that all of the trials of this lifetime and others will be healed and integrated into wholeness as well. May knowing you are not doing this alone bring you peace. For I am with you in love, peace and harmony."

Day 281 — Archangel Ariel

"You are doing most beautifully our friend. You have weathered many troubled times and have come through the other side safely and in good hands. Your noble cause will not be forgotten. You are a Divine Messenger here on earth helping to bring God's light and love to the many who have forgotten that God's Grace is always available to them upon request. Your light has become brighter. What you wish for will come true. Allow yourself to rest some more and then we'd like you to discover more play in your life. What makes your heart sing like the most beautiful song bird you've ever heard. Be in that wonder more. You deserve that time for yourself. All of God's bounty is yours. Enjoy it. Revel in it and receive the gift of life that has been given unto you. Your day is right now. Your blessings are here and plentiful. May you know how absolutely cherished and loved you are. God's Grace is yours forever."

Notes, inspired writing or other brainstorming ideas...

Day 282 – Archangel Michael

"Your health matters and is at the forefront of how you feel daily. Recharging your batteries when prompted brings in higher level healing teams of assistance for you as you call me in while you lay down. In truth, there is nothing more important than your good health. How you perceive the world is filtered through the lens of how good you feel on any particular day. Making this a top priority will help others follow in your example. You are a leader by nature and loving yourself into vibrant health helps us assist those around you who look up to you come into equilibrium again also. You matter. We are caring for you daily with light being brought unto your body systems. Claiming a healthy body, mind and soul for yourself ushers in new beginnings of longevity for those loved ones you care dearly about. You are being honored today for your courage. May your strength and determination continue to light the way for others."

Notes, inspired writing or other brainstorming ideas...

Day 283 — Archangel Raphael

"Healing begins by asking for assistance with letting go of strongholds that seemed gripping to you sometimes. These internal urges to gravitate towards that which may not be very good for you leads you out of center places with yourself. To get back to center stage and in good graces with yourself again it helps to not be pressed for "making things right". To allow is better than following the urge to fix. In the fixing you lose, in the fixing you heal. What needs healing doesn't need fixing, it only needs loving yourself enough to take a rain check on the need to fix anything that is broken. It is in the broken pieces the ultimate Divine Healing of the soul happens."

Notes, inspired writing or other brainstorming ideas...

Day 284 — Archangel Michael

"When judgment happens it leads you outside of yourself into fear. Fear of the unknown and fear of great change. We'd like you to know that all is in Divine Order. The precise elements will be occurring at the exact right Divine time for all involved. What is yesteryear's news does not need to be your concern, let that be for others to wallow in. Your focus is in the Divine Magical moments unfolding before you in joyous splendor. What held you back in past lives will not do so in this one. You are working with us and your soul to ensure this. Your light is a beacon in the night, let it shine, let it shine."

Notes, inspired writing or other brainstorming ideas . . .

Day 285 — Archangel Gabriel

"Believe in yourself through and through. You have a team of Angelic guidance all throughout the day. Ask for your Soul's Purpose blueprints to be brought in for you all the way. You have not failed at anything. Do not allow these voices in your head to take hold. Your ideas are too important to squelch them right from the gate. Your ideas, inventions and creations are worthy for the world to see. Let the world behold them and hold nothing back. You have nothing to lose, we assure you of this. What do you want to be remembered for? Go forth and be that in your internal dialogue and with your thinking processes. You already ARE that from your soul's perspective. You are that which you think yourself to be. Amen."

Notes, inspired writing or other brainstorming ideas...

Day 286 – Archangel Michael

"When others want your attention, know they are like little children who are desperately seeking love to nurture and refill them with the light of Divinity. Some will try anything to receive more of heaven's light. When this happens to you, call Mother Mary in. She is always available for those are in need of the energy of Mother's love. You may also call me in to un-cord you from those who are seeking your time and attention when you are feeling like you need to replenish and refill yourself. Mother Mary wants you to know you do not need to try to please everyone. Communing with Mother Earth will bring balance back into your energy system again and recharge your batteries. You may invite others to do the same, as you call Mother Mary in to assist you and the other. Take a deep breath. Ask your body what it needs most right now and listen for the answer from within. Mother Mary and I bring you peace, love, longevity and God's connecting light through eternity. And so it is."

Notes, inspired writing or other brainstorming ideas...

Day 287 – Archangel Ariel

"Be strong and know your pathway is being aligned for you and succinctly connected to God's light and your Divine Destiny Soul's purpose as you pray daily for our assistance with anything that should arise. You have already won the battle, our Dearly Beloved. The fight has not been lost, it is already triumphant and complete. Let your light shine until the end of time and beyond. Your return home has been ensured and wrapped in God's Love for you. What brings you peace, ushers God's peace into Mother Earth's belly. Behold and know that God's power source has arrived and will never forsake you. Let this ring peace into all of your cells in your body. For it is your time to shine, this day forevermore."

Notes, inspired writing or other brainstorming ideas...

Day 288 – Archangel Michael

"You are indeed a bright and shining warrior soul. You have not lost anything, but have arrived at the most profound earth experience ever lived. We stand from the mountain tops watching over you and your mission on earth. You are a deliverer of the order of truth of the highest accord. Claim God's light upon the earth wherever you travel. I will meet you there and deliver unto you and all the people God calls, for the time of awakening light is here. What seems lost, has not been. This is the moment to deliver God's bounty to the earth. What seems weak is being made strong. Let your light be a beacon in the light, for many lost souls need this desperately. You are a deliverer of my light and you have the backing of all my warrior angels behind you. Go forth and bring God's bountiful light to the earth and her people and so shall your bounty of your heavenly riches be delivered unto you."

Notes, inspired writing or other brainstorming ideas...

Day 289 — Archangel Gabriel

"We thank you for your most endearing service upon the earth in the utmost humbleness. You listen for the call daily as to where and what you are guided to do and we thank you for this. We are transforming any of the old poverty consciousness thought forms for you, so that you may see God's bountiful abundance and prosperity that is available for you everywhere. Your heart is being made whole again, our dearly beloved friend. In the riches of the earth's treasures let the old pain, fear and feelings of abandonment be washed away with each sunlit day and be replaced by the fruits of the seeds you have already sewn. All that is required now is to simply enjoy and receive massive amounts of God's love that is being poured into your body, mind, heart and soul for the rest of your earthly years. Indeed your service has already been remembered and honored by the heavenly kingdom."

Notes, inspired writing or other brainstorming ideas...

Day 290 — Archangel Michael

"The love of you knows you are always connected to what will work best for you. If your stomach feels queasy there are higher, more viable solutions for everyone at hand. The river has endless abundant channels of connected opportunities of expansion. Choose the ones that feel refreshing, like a clear blue waterfall to your body, mind and soul."

Notes, inspired writing or other brainstorming ideas...

Day 291 – Archangel Jophiel

"Lead by connecting into the highest level of light possible for yourself. When you do all the illusion falls away. Your next step becomes clearer and clearer each day. Staying in the trenches is not safety. Before making a decision ask me and the other Archangels to surround you with our light of clarity and peace. From here all decisions you make will be choices that raise you up higher in all aspects of your light. When you ask, we are able to reach you. Be at peace in knowing this is true. You have our assistance until the end of time and beyond. Rest assured when you sleep we are also with you. Sleep sweet… we are but a request away."

Notes, inspired writing or other brainstorming ideas…

Day 292 – Archangel Michael

"Celebrating the moment creates sparks of joy that last a lifetime. You are guided, protected and loved in a multitude of ways. What brings you the most joy frees your heart and soul. Believe you are making a difference, because you are. Write down what you want help with the most because your resources are expanding now."

Notes, inspired writing or other brainstorming ideas...

Day 293 — Archangel Uriel

"When you let go, surrendering any worries we can more easily bring you pleasant surprises that await. Being in a state of peace brings many miracles from the Angelic realms. Picture us working miracles for you behind the scenes. This gives us permission to bring them to you. Infinite blessings of joy await."

Notes, inspired writing or other brainstorming ideas...

Day 294 – Archangel Michael

"You are your best self when you take care of and honor yourself in every way possible. What brings a smile to your beautiful face, does to ours as well. You have love to give, yes? How large is your receiving container? Bring that balance back to you so that you have the ability to receive at even broader capacities. You have the right to change your mind at anytime. The people that are connected to you can then receive all of the Divine Goodness waiting to rush into their lives with more ease."

Notes, inspired writing or other brainstorming ideas...

Day 295 – Archangel Chamuel

"To be given a heads up about things coming up in your life would spoil the precious moments of love shared with those you are about to encounter. Whether you deem your experience troublesome in surprising moments or exuberant, either way there is love to be shared amongst souls who may be needing a desperate reminder that they too are loved. There is refuge in knowing we back you with great love beyond logical comprehension. When things seem unresolvable is when they have the most resolution ready to anchor in. I am here to help you see the cracks in the doors most needed for you to open. For there waiting is the greatest love of all ready for your light to fill it."

Notes, inspired writing or other brainstorming ideas...

Day 296 – Archangel Michael

"Be still and behold the beauty of the transformation that is happening within you. We feel like proud parents for how far you have come in your earth school journey. Remember to be kind to yourself with every thought and deed. More blessings are being sent your way that will put a joyous smile on your face."

Notes, inspired writing or other brainstorming ideas...

Day 297 – Archangel Gabriel

"Give yourself a break and have fun with it all. New ways of doing things are being shown to you today. All is possible and even more potential exists with a lighthearted playful stance. You are appreciated for your willingness to show up every day. We are standing right next to you giving you rays of Divine Inspiration. All will be revealed through not taking any of it too seriously and enjoying what feels most uplifting for you to do."

Notes, inspired writing or other brainstorming ideas...

Day 298 — Archangel Michael

"When you feel misunderstood it is an opportunity to heal old traumas. Ask us to transform these trigger points into your highest life purpose blueprints and so shall it be. No longer does the pain need to define you. What heals you heals all. Others do take note, even if they verbally refrain. We commend you for being willing to transform what you thought was you, into the pure, crystal clear sparkling expression of who your soul already is."

Notes, inspired writing or other brainstorming ideas...

Day 299 — Archangel Uriel

"Simple is the word for today. Things can be much simpler for you now. What you intend can happen as you continue to allow the old beliefs about who you thought you were to be transformed. Your magical life is here, right in front of you, all around you and is brilliantly calling you to enjoy the simple pleasures. All is well."

Notes, inspired writing or other brainstorming ideas...

Day 300 — Archangel Michael

"Your vulnerability makes you accessible to those who are yearning to dive into the healing waters within themselves. What you speak from your heart's perspective could trigger others and cause them to feel uncomfortable. We still encourage you to speak your truth as inspired to because what would be beneficial to come to the surface for healing for one will do on the same root issue for many. Being vulnerable allows us the opportunity to shine light on the tender points that once caused you pain so the resistance can be transformed into soul-shine."

Notes, inspired writing or other brainstorming ideas...

Day 301 – Archangel Raphael

"The Universe and the Angelic Realm will always support your dreams being born into physical reality. You have come here to birth them. The alignment process begins with shifting out what no longer serves you or feels good any longer. As this occurs there will be a space for new frequencies or blueprints to come in. Call upon me to help make room for these new blueprints to anchor in. I will help in the restructuring process as the old is released. You are such a beautiful being of light. Let this process be simple and easy, for it can be."

Notes, inspired writing or other brainstorming ideas...

Day 302 – Archangel Michael

"Celebrating the moment creates sparks of joy that last a lifetime. You are guided, protected and loved in a multitude of ways. What brings you the most joy frees your heart and soul. Believe you are making a difference, because you are. Write down what you want help with the most because your resources are expanding now."

Notes, inspired writing or other brainstorming ideas...

Day 303 — Archangel Gabriel

"Your desires are a lovely reflection of how much you want to serve humanity with the gift of who you are. Set yourself free by diving into these creations. They will bring connection points to those who are waiting for them. We support you in this and are delighted to energize your creations with light, blessings and love from all of the Angelic Realm."

Notes, inspired writing or other brainstorming ideas...

Day 304 – Archangel Michael

"Your intentions are strong. All of the angelic realm and myself are supporting your dreams, desires, goals and aspirations. Whenever you call my name for more protection, support, upliftment or love I am there with you, by your side giving you strength, stability, love and understanding. What you want is within reach, believe this. Call upon me to further clear the way for your dreams to come into full fruition. I am eternally at your service. Be well."

Notes, inspired writing or other brainstorming ideas...

Day 305 – Archangel Jeremiel

"There is plenty of time for all that you want. Enjoy this present moment to the fullest. Dream about what you'd like to happen and let go of forcing it into being. Your joy in this now moment brings it to you faster than anything else. You are cherished for bringing more joy to the planet."

Notes, inspired writing or other brainstorming ideas...

Day 306 – Archangel Michael

"The superhero in you knows your power. Asking us to turn what ails you into your superpower is where you begin reclaiming your God-given power. Your superpower is your soul's calling. You came to earth to bring your superpower to the world without compromise. What serves the world for the greater good combined with your dharma or your soul's natural and innate gifts is your superpower. If you say Yes, all of the Archangels and myself will be activating your superpower for you today and while you sleep. Once your dharma, your Soul's Divine Mission is fully activated you will be an unstoppable force for good."

Notes, inspired writing or other brainstorming ideas...

Day 307 – Archangel Raphael

"If your energy reserves are low on any given day, call me in, I am here for you. Ask me to lift worry from your thoughts. What feels heavy to you can be transformed into feeling much lighter. Tonight as you sleep I will bring you a new way of looking at the situation at hand if you'd like. This way your body, mind and spirit can restore itself more efficiently through the peace and healing I bring you today and during your slumber. What seems like a detriment may be a blessing in disguise. There is no need to fret. Only to connect to the greater you that is overseeing your journey on earth. Your soul connects with us frequently for updates on what may work better for you. You have an entire team of advisors guiding your every step. We are strengthening your energy reserves right now. Be at peace and know that all is well."

Notes, inspired writing or other brainstorming ideas...

Day 308 — Archangel Michael

"Nature delivers to you signs and messages along your path daily if you will watch for them. For instance, if you saw a bear enter your world, this could be a very loud message to listen from within more adherently. A bear's warning is to claim what's yours and don't stop just because others do not have the same beliefs as you. You are a most diligent messenger of light as you forage your path and heed the early warning signals that arrive to steer you closer to home. Your homeland inside of your heart holds within it all the answers you seek. One does not need to seek approvals from those who do not have the same mission that you do. What helps you spread your wings is to listen to your own heartbeat for signals. What your heart knows is true for you… IS."

Notes, inspired writing or other brainstorming ideas...

Day 309 – Archangel Ariel

"Nature's way is leading you to all the abundance you've ever dreamed of in alignment with your Soul's Destiny. Where you have been led to go, others may not understand, yet in order to go in that direction what propels you forward is trusting that internal voice that says, "Go here, look over there, research this…" The voice that is for your highest and best good will always feel like love. Where you get misaligned is by not heeding the earliest of signals of where to go and what choices ARE in fact for your best interest. Ask us to clear away all the old programming that would get in the way of this. In doing so, you'll discover double and triple rainbows on the other side of the hill. Divinity knows your Grandness. Your disbelief in self serves no one. Your sincere desire to serve the greater good in such a way that feels like freedom and love for your heart is where you'll feel the entire Universe assisting your mission and uplifting all who meet your path."

Notes, inspired writing or other brainstorming ideas...

Day 310 — Archangel Michael

"Behold a newly created Divine Day has arrived for you. What are you wishing you had more of? Picture this now and visualize this wrapped in my light. Feel, sense or see this area of your life transforming into something even better. What does that look like and feel like now? Let the blessings continue to unfold for you inside of God's Grace. For it is in God's Grace that all that was thought impossible is made whole and real. Go forth into the eternity of your life and pronounce all that you love to the world and amongst your circle of friends. The ones that are for what you love will be reaching and sustaining new heights with you. Celebrate your love shining forth in all the glory hours of your day."

Notes, inspired writing or other brainstorming ideas...

Day 311 – Archangel Raphael

"After a long day it helps your body restore equilibrium by laying horizontal. Laying in the horizontal position, even before bed time helps stress and the adrenals from being over-activated. Choose inspiring books to read in bed, or watch informative, educational, calm and peaceful videos while laying down before bedtime if you find you cannot fall asleep right away. Preferably it is better to not have electrical devices on while you sleep in the bedroom. Before going to sleep you may call me in to restore your body and rejuvenate any areas that need healing. More Divine healing wisdom will also be imparted to you by me while you sleep by asking for healing from me upon retiring for the evening. It is an honor to serve you in this way and heal not only your physical body, but recharge your light body with healing light from the heavens."

Notes, inspired writing or other brainstorming ideas...

Day 312 — Archangel Michael

"When you feel in a lull, keep in mind how much integration of higher frequencies are going on behind the scenes. If you have been working with us for any length of time, the upgraded levels of frequencies having been shifting your perception and your entire life's framework. This is why the direction of your life may shift several times over in just a few short years. As the God Codes and your new Soul's Purpose blueprints come in, you may feel out of sorts, like you are processing things from deep within. Taking naps when this is happening is a really wonderful way to integrate the new light frequencies we are sending you. Also, gardening and spending time outdoors with your bare feet upon the earth and your heart open to the sky and the trees brings in a flood of awareness from us that deeply root the new Wisdom for the Ages within you. We thank you for your willingness to work with us in this way. It is through your Graceful receiving that more anchor points for upgraded revolutionary ways of being are able to be planted through love."

Notes, inspired writing or other brainstorming ideas...

Day 313 – Archangel Ariel

"Your prayers are heard immediately by God, by the Creator, by the Divine, by all the Archangels, all the Angels of heaven and Ascended Masters. There are delegation Angels that help deliver your prayers to God's helpers in spirit who can assist you the most. What helps bridge the gap the most from the light that's in the etheric to the physical earth receiving light is your prayers. Prayers create a cosmic opening to God. It is through prayer that Divine Frequencies from God can be sent. The Angels celebrate every time a prayer is said by you, did you know that? It is exquisitely delightful for Angels to receive prayers, for this gives them permission to assist. There are 1000's of Angels waiting for prayers right now. Angels that assist the earth wait for them. Your prayers are delivered to them the second they are said. What is it you most need assistance with today? Say a prayer from your heart right now requesting anything you need help with and be open for miraculous events to take place."

Notes, inspired writing or other brainstorming ideas...

Day 314 - Archangel Michael

"When you feel entrapped or hooked in by someone else's comment, it is important to realize that at the base of it, they are usually just in dire need of love. When the feelings of lack and "why me" are surfacing for them, the best thing you can do is not get hooked into their constricting thoughts of how things are. In fact, there are most often a multitude of dynamic solutions on the way to them. Pray that they be open to receiving all that is good for them and that any obstacles that are in the way be removed completely. Often when someone has lost hope it can feel like no resources are available that would truly work for them. We'd like you to know just how much your prayers assist in opening these doors of solutions for others, so that they may receive the very best in miraculous healing and resolutions available. Keep sending your prayers to us so that all the Angels waiting for permission to come in and help, can go to work right away on delivering miracles to the doors of those who need them the most."

Notes, inspired writing or other brainstorming ideas...

Day 315 – Archangel Metatron

"As you are in a state of pure creative love, in song, in harmony with your highest Destiny Path, this can be felt by those who know you across the continents. Continuing to ask that your most fun, sweet, adventurous Soul's Calling be designed for you by us creates a non resistant state of being. In this type of buzzing like a hummingbird energy, because life is a miracle itself, you are sending out waves of frequencies to all of humanity and to those who know you now that something "more" is possible for them also, you see? You having the smallest of organic, joy buzzing moments in your day such as watching the sunrise or set you set into motion infinite possibilities for others to follow that example. What's possible for you when you are emanating the purest form of light that creates outstanding possibilities to be made available for others? First these options are shown to them on the etheric levels they also reside in. Then here in the physical they suddenly feel an opening, a shift, like something has changed for the better. This is what you bringing in more joy does, in the swiftest of moments sometimes. We appreciate you aiming for pure, raw life enhancing bliss. Behold, there will be a day when all humans everywhere will be experiencing this as a synchronistic way of experiencing their every day."

Notes, inspired writing or other brainstorming ideas...

Day 316 – Archangel Michael

"When another truffles your step, this is a sure sign there is still a tie of some sort there between the two of you. This entwinement may not be absolutely healthy for you. If this is your gut feeling, ask me to bring you resolution on this matter while you sleep. We will do energy work together on the inner dimensions of light so that what has yanked your chain in the past can no longer do so. Us releasing that which is pulling on you from the other assists in releasing and healing other aspects of yourself that can sometimes get disturbed by this. Know that your gut instinct is usually right. If the energy feels constrictive to you in any way I invite you to call me in to release the energetic constraints that may be happening. Your well being may very well depend on this. If the early warning signals are not heeded more strongholds can sometimes end up throwing the most diligent Divine Light Carriers off kilter. You are very strong and your soul is very wise. Asking for assistance when needed is a sign of strength, not weakness. Always at your service."

Notes, inspired writing or other brainstorming ideas . . .

Day 317 – Archangel Ariel

"We congratulate you, for you have made it past the old stronghold of people-pleasing for the sake of receiving love. You now know your love comes through for you like pure spring water on a fresh summer day. Picture, feel and sense the most beautiful light you can imagine flowing from the heavens pouring down into you. Allow God's light, Your Divine Creator's light to penetrate all of your cells, all of your being-ness. Be one with this light now, feeling the uplifting strength of Divine support that pours like a summer waterfall in through your crown chakra. Let this light liquefy anything that is bothering you, feeling all concerns be bathed in the glory of The Creator's love for you. Feel yourself being held by the hands of God. The outpouring of Divine Love for you is always flowing, never ending, always continuing with more goodness for your life. What once seemed so far away, is very close. Divine assistance is forever at hand, and so it is."

Notes, inspired writing or other brainstorming ideas...

Day 318 – Archangel Raphael

"Know that your light is shining brighter now. The more you call us in, the more we can assist your clarity levels. You are doing beautifully on the etheric realms with asking for higher, more supportive blueprints to come in for you and your loved ones. It's working! You have relaxed nicely into more of a Divine flow for your life. We send you today more healing for your heart, so it may be strengthened even more with emerald crystalline energy from us. What helps your situation get even better is to continue connecting to Mother Earth daily and calling us in to brighten every aspect of your day. If you could only see how beautiful you are on the etheric realms, you'd be in awe with how breathtaking your light is that shines forth through you here in the physical. Be willing for it to get even better and it will."

Notes, inspired writing or other brainstorming ideas...

Day 319 – Archangel Ariel

"Continue to pray for the entire earth every day and all who are suffering, that their pain may be healed completely by God's light. This unprecedented time on earth needs your prayers. As the new levels of light are flooding into the earth's atmosphere and core from us and all of the Ascended Masters, your prayers help others find the light more easily. Pray that the suffering be released for all people and that the holy light be brought to those who are seeking, including yourself. This helps release strongholds that have been here for eons of time. Thank you for helping us bring the new form energy to earth, as the old crumbles. The outworn structures are supposed to be washed away so the light of the heavens continue to be anchored in so that the goodwill for all continues to take form."

Notes, inspired writing or other brainstorming ideas...

Day 320 – Archangel Michael

"When another thinks you "should" be doing something, you know deep down inside your soul is not for you, call me in with my sword to clear all the distortion energy away that may be trying to clutter your clear thinking. There are a lot of forces on earth that no longer have a hold of those that are working in Divine Light each day. When energy around you does not feel like love, but more like control, call us in to assist you with releasing from your world all that is not lifting you higher. What ascends you to your next level will never feel like control, it will always feel loving, sweet and nurturing to your body, mind and soul. You have made it through many veils of illusion. What feels good to your soul's essence is good. What feels bad to you usually will not help you expand into all the light that is you more fully. Forgive them, they know not what they do. What would you like assistance with today? Ask and ye shall receive. Play, laugh, have fun in nature. We are within you raising you higher as you do."

Notes, inspired writing or other brainstorming ideas...

Day 321 — Archangel Gabriel

"You are not supposed to struggle any longer. Yes, giving birth to new creations can feel like a birthing process, this is normal, but now is the time for you to feel loved and supported with all the ideas you are being given. We are sending you frequencies today for your creative ideas and projects — that they be surrounded in light and frequencies of love. That they reach the audience they are meant to bless. Cheers to your creative endeavors! For without them the world would not be the same."

Notes, inspired writing or other brainstorming ideas...

Day 322 – Archangel Michael

"We are sending you frequencies right now of rejuvenation, love, joy and sweetness from our hearts into yours. We place a smile upon your heart. Breathe this in, for your heart's energy is being lit up with your eternal flame even brighter. This sacred flame inside your heart can never be extinguished and is connected to your sacred journey blueprint. Your sacred journey blueprint has been blessed by us, along with embodying Mother and Father God's blessings upon it. Spending sacred moments communing with your sacred heart daily nourishes your vital organs and thoughts and wakes up other parts of yourself in the process. Your sacred heart is a magnetic creator for all that is good and all that is absolutely nurturing for your body, mind and soul. What you create from this space is infinite possibilities and rainbows of happy times ahead."

Notes, inspired writing or other brainstorming ideas . . .

Day 323 — Archangel Ariel

"We are sending you frequencies today to shift out of the outworn routines more easily. There are new energetic pathways being created from the higher realms into the earth by us so that a lot of what was impossible before is available now. When you align to these higher frequencies being sent by us, you are in the flow of a stream of consciousness that contains ideas that make transformation doable. When you go out of your mind's logical thought processing during meditation, or while enjoying the beautiful weather or sunshine, call us in and we will flood beams of light into you and your surroundings. Think of this as angel light baths, for they are very powerful and real. Enjoy them to the fullest."

Notes, inspired writing or other brainstorming ideas...

Day 324 – Archangel Uriel

"The global shifts and releasing will be continuing for quite some time. Your inner stability and connection to a sound stream of grounding frequencies are available as you need them. Take a deep breath right now and feel these stabilizing frequencies I bring you in through your crown chakra. Centering yourself in this vibration daily helps all those around you feel more peace and security. The fluctuations will continue on earth as she releases what she no longer needs from her belly. You help her as you allow us to send you frequencies of cosmic stabilizing light. Thank you for your participation with bringing this light through for all."

Notes, inspired writing or other brainstorming ideas...

Day 325 – Archangel Gabriel

"Never say never is key. Yet to know thyself and your sacred journey upon life holds relevance for an eternity. Little compromises here and there impede your sacred journey. What blesses your sacred walk upon the earth is a knowingness of what's right for you. The blessings upon you are in the multitudes. What brings your body, mind and soul deep peace delivers blessings upon blessings to your door. Your sacred life journey is always unfolding, yet when you are fully in the flow of it, not much can make you hit the guardrails any longer. What is truth for you is felt in every fiber of your being. What makes your cells younger with vibrant herbal tonics and living foods makes your brain resilient. We call in now all that is good for you. May you be enriched by our refueling flowers at your feet."

Notes, inspired writing or other brainstorming ideas...

Day 326 – Archangel Michael

"Many of you are going through feelings of jet lag, even though you are not flying on a plane. This is due to the pivotal shifts the earth is making right now. If you are feeling contracted in the mornings and not very inspired we invite you to lay down upon Mother Earth on your back and with bare feet for 30 minutes and gaze at the sky or the trees. Through the heartbeat of Mother Earth your heart beat is synchronized with hers. Ask her to heal the pain and call us in each morning. You can do this and you'll feel your own body rhythms beginning to reach heightened joy states more naturally. When you are in love with what you are feeling by taking as many nature breaks as you can possibly get in, the joy shines through with a vibrant array of frequencies that create ring waves of love that wrap the globe through your loving intentions."

Notes, inspired writing or other brainstorming ideas...

Day 327 – Archangel Metatron

"Health issues sometimes get in the way of one fully living their Divine Soul's Calling upon the earth. We suggest you heal yourself first; call in as much healing and guidance for your own healing as needed until you feel full of life force energy enough to bring your creations to the world. If your vibrancy or health is off balance, this may be the very thing you need to attend to first, before your Soul will enhance your Divine Destiny Blueprints all the way, you see? Your soul always wants you to take the best care of you first and so do we. It is never advisable to give and then give some more until you are utterly depleted. Build your reserves. Eat fresh healing herbs and foods. Wallow in nature until you are breathing vitality into every pore and cell of your being. As you refill and recharge, new ideas for prosperity living will be delivered to you with every healing breath you take. Your soul may want you to make a pivotal shift with your health so that you have enough sustenance and reserves to live at your highest destiny blueprint possible. Research organic, nutritious food sources so you can ingest and assimilate the foods that would be best for your body systems. Health comes first, then more of your Divine Destiny Blueprints will arrive at moments of awakening while pondering what you love about your life while in sublime bliss in nature's caress."

Notes, inspired writing or other brainstorming ideas...

Day 328 – Archangel Jeremiel

"We smooth out your feathers today from anything that has ruffled them recently. Sometimes the antagonists are our greatest teachers. The intuitive wisdom that you hold inside all of your being is the wisdom you have been seeking on earth for ages. What frees you the most is knowing you have it all from within. All the abundance, good health, love, joy, peace and prosperity can first be found inside the core essence of you. Even if all has been lost, that Divine core essence can still be found. The fiber of your being is of goodness. Your Divine nature is a never ending pulse of goodness, grace, love and abundance. We send you waves of harmonizing energy today and tonight while you sleep. What floods you with love for an eternity is what we gift you with through God's Grace. You are worthy of this and more. And so it is."

Notes, inspired writing or other brainstorming ideas...

Day 329 – Archangel Ariel

"Be bold, be you. Please don't shy away from the success that is yours. Be rich in your morals. Treasure the open air. Stay centered in knowing how worthy you are, our dearly beloved. What ails you, you are not alone with. Freedom comes from exhaling with the breeze and driving off into the sunset. Be that which you came here to be. Be all of you. Be brave. You have this and we have your hand through thick and thin."

Notes, inspired writing or other brainstorming ideas...

Day 330 – Archangel Gabriel

"Reducing the unnecessary stress in your life brings you peace of mind. Close your eyes if you'd like… Where in your life are you holding tension or extra stress? Energetically place this area of your life into a ball of golden and white light that we have created especially for you today. Allow yourself to let go of tension around this now. Transformation and more support are being sent to you for this area. Allow yourself to be free from worry, even if just for a moment at a time. You are a wondrous child of the Divine. Your smile matters to us, for this is what is most important."

Notes, inspired writing or other brainstorming ideas...

Day 331 – Archangel Raphael

"Nature's grace is her ability to heal your body, mind and soul. Her aim is ultimately always healing. After storms come rebirth. What part of your life would you like a rebirth with? Picture, feel or sense this now. Allow the love of you to know that it is possible through requesting it and by listening at Divine synchronicity's doorstep. Think about something from your past that seemed impossible, yet looking back you realize you got through it and a rebirth happened. The gentleness of rebirths can also be requested. What helps you transition smoothly into your next levels of awareness and into Divine Express is being willing to let go of what's not working very well and exchange them in for cascades of love and blessings upon your life. We strengthen your willingness to release what drags you down and ask for higher assistance here. Where you feel weak will you will be made strong. The lighter blueprints for your life, health, longevity and awareness are being ushered in now as you say Yes. May you know how much we cherish you and your commitment to be here."

Notes, inspired writing or other brainstorming ideas...

Day 332 – Archangel Michael

"If something feels like a complete turn off to you, listen to this. That is your soul speaking to you in the language of what is for your highest and best good and what is not. When you get a turned upside down feeling in your stomach that is telling you to not head in that direction. Things may change later, but for now that is not the direction that will lift you higher and it may prove to drag you down should you move into that current. This may not always make sense to your logical mind, often times it does not. What hurts you often turns your stomach way ahead of time. Consider this a warning bell inside your solar plexus area. What propels you forward with feelings of freedom, sweetness, purity, wholeness and clear expansive thinking is what is being presented to you as a better choice in the matter. Allow your decision making ability to feel its way into things or say no thank you to them. What is for your highest and best good will always feel like light with no constraints or restrictions attached."

Notes, inspired writing or other brainstorming ideas...

Day 333 – Archangel Gabriel

"People all over the world are becoming increasingly aware of the subtle energies they are made of and that are in their environment. It will be increasingly important as the months and years arrive to learn about what brings you energy and builds energy reserves in your body, mind and soul and what is truly depleting it. Detoxifying the body and then adding vital minerals and nutrients back in increases your awareness of what breathes life into you and what drains it from you. Request more of what nourishes you from the inside out. What will bring you more vitality, vital life force energy? Listen for the answer. You may also be receiving signs and messages from me today in unexpected ways if you say yes and you would like them. I am always happy to bring you more clues and support with what will help sustain your beautiful life here upon the planet even better."

Notes, inspired writing or other brainstorming ideas...

Day 334 – Archangel Azriel

"We are so proud of you for believing in yourself more. Challenging yourself with endeavors that grow you assist you in unveiling the depths of why you are here in the first place. To reveal what's behind each curtain and see if it is for you or not shows how willing you are to explore leading edge ways of not only improving your life, but the lives of others. To uncover what may work better leads to cutting edge ways of living that we present to you in your dreams and in the ideas that pop into your consciousness. Write down your ideas because more are on their way. As soon as you get your notebook out to write one day, another leading edge discovery is in the works for you that is a part of your Soul's Purpose, Your Divine Destiny here upon the earth. To write them down is the first step in revealing the hidden wisdom that each one has for you. Trust what you are receiving from us. What you have wanted for your life is unfolding at quantum speed."

Notes, inspired writing or other brainstorming ideas...

Day 335 – Archangel Ariel

"Standing in your power can be a gentle act of loving kindness for yourself and all involved. Guilt is never needed when it is time to allow your Divine Authentic Power through. Those that witness your loving firmness with what you need take heed and understand how to be authentically real to themselves as well. Allowing the highest and best good in can be empowering and freeing for those willing to go with the flow of Divine Grace in order. You have divinely accepted grace's help. In doing so your life will continue to flourish."

Notes, inspired writing or other brainstorming ideas...

Day 336 – Archangel Metatron

"Be willing to take a stand for what you want and need in order to thrive. This is where help from us and the Divine can reach in and bring countless blessings to you and everyone who is dear to your heart. You have made it past the point of merely surviving to an elevated state of higher frequencies of light. You no longer need to lean on any one person too much as you allow Divine Light in daily to lift you up. Further light code structures of peace, joy, abundance, prosperity, grace and authentic happiness are here to stay for you. Ask for more of this light each morning from us and get ready for waterfalls of Divine Treasures to activate more blessings coming your way. You are worthy my friend. You always have been. In your dreams you meet with us to discuss your life. It is time to know your worthiness in your waking hours, for it is through you we are flooding Divine Light to Mother Earth and all of her people. We are honored to do this as you say Yes to receiving more Divine Light from us. Let it be known how much we adore you. When you claim Mother God and Father God's Light as yours, this allows us to usher in floods of Divine Treasures for humanity."

Notes, inspired writing or other brainstorming ideas...

Day 337 – Archangel Ariel

"As you need a break from all of the people, places, ways of the world call upon me to silence the noise of the outside world for you. For this is one of my many specialties. Take a dip in the ocean waters or lie upon Mother Earth's breathing surface. What you'll find there is me with you, calming the storms around you so you may take a much needed nature breather. In doing so, allow us to renew your heart, body, mind and soul. Your worthiness of this has never been in question by us. What restores you helps all of the beloved animals ascend to new heights along with you. Abundant and beautiful bounty is here for all. Will you partake of Mother Nature's gift for you today? We touch your cheek and chin with a sweet caress for the brave soul that you are. Let your heart enjoy the taste of sweet surrender today in the bosom of Divine Mother's heartbeat, singing lullaby hymns to your restful mind."

Notes, inspired writing or other brainstorming ideas...

Day 338 – Archangel Raphael

"When you seek love only from another human and forget to knock on the doors of heaven, the welcoming entryway of the Divine, you have forgotten who you are and where you came from. What keeps the atoms and molecules alive and dancing in synergistic particle form is the light from your beautiful Creator, whom your soul was born from. That which you are has never left you. The grandness of you always exists and lives on forever. Allow this eternal light to lift your heart unto heaven's gate today. The atoms and molecules of you is made from the same particles that stardust comes from. Place your wish inside your heart now and we will bless your wish and your heart while you sleep with our Divine Mother and Father's everlasting love for you. Expect something even better to be delivered. What you yearn for is available and on its way to you now."

Notes, inspired writing or other brainstorming ideas...

Day 339 – Archangel Ariel

"When you love something sometimes it's better to set it free instead of forcing love to be a certain way. Love has no container and is never ending and ever beginning. What once worked a very long time ago may not be feasible in today's world. Your heart is grouped together with your soul family and has never been apart from them really. It is only the illusion of separateness that brings pain. Give yourself a much needed respite here and know your divinity lives on forever and so does theirs."

Notes, inspired writing or other brainstorming ideas...

Day 340 – Archangel Metatron

"Sometimes I see many of you having so many choices you do not know which ones to energize or where to place your energy, thoughts and focus into. We'd like you to know you cannot make a wrong choice here; however, some choices are just the long way around and some have shorter routes to your heart's desires. Place 2-3 choices before you right now that you are considering and I will energize it with my light. Ask each choice which one brings you the most buoyancy, joy, freedom, love and puts a smile on your face. Go with this one. By going with the one that brings a smile to your face you will always get it right."

Notes, inspired writing or other brainstorming ideas...

Day 341 – Archangel Gabriel

"When creative inspiration hits, take it as a sign that expanded soul purpose blueprints have been given to you by us and your soul. These blueprints hold within them a few to several options for you that could expand if you'd like them to. Try some of them on for size and see which ones feel better to you. You don't need to act on them just yet. Be willing to ponder them for a while and even write down as many ideas in your notebook that come to you. Give yourself a week to years if needed to see if the idea still holds a "charge" of light for you that says, YES! If one does, then move forward with thoughtful footing and if need be ask others who have skills in areas you may not, to assist you. This helps balance out what can carry your soul blueprints forward. Also, ask me to energize for you the blueprints that feel the most vibrant to you. This is my specialty and it is an honor for us to bless them for you. We salute you on your earth journey. You are well on your way to your most joyous heart giving self. You are beaming."

Notes, inspired writing or other brainstorming ideas...

Day 342 — Archangel Ariel

"Be patient with the process you are undergoing right now. The change you want is happening and we commend you with how forthcoming you are with assisting it along quite nicely. If you were to speed up time to the point you want to be you would have missed the most cherished opportunities of experiencing Divine Mother bless every moment of your life. Not just the great accomplishments, but the seemingly mundane daily happenings you stumble upon. Relishing in the simple moments allows us to water the seeds that have been planted for you. Time to nourish the soil now with water, sunlight and tender loving care. We'll meet you there."

Notes, inspired writing or other brainstorming ideas...

Day 343 – Archangel Raphael

"Your Divine Destiny has arrived. You are a shining light amongst your friends and peers. You make us smile. Relax a little more in knowing you ARE doing a good job. Allow trying too hard to be replaced with enjoying every minute of it. The discovery is the most important part of what you are doing. When you are in struggle or angst, try opening your palms and remembering your strength comes from your soul. You do not need to muscle your strength for all of your activities. You have arrived because you have crossed the threshold of self doubt into your soul's mission. Allow your soul's calling to carry you forth and ride that most adventuresome ride all the way to the promised land. You got this through and through. The hardest part has already been won."

Notes, inspired writing or other brainstorming ideas...

Day 344 – Archangel Jophiel

"The hand of God is upon you now. Allow the seemingly unending pain to be purified, cleansed and healed completely by God's powerful love for you that has been unwavering all of your lifetimes upon the earth. You have indeed been a treasure to humanity and let it be known that any suffering you have endured has been remedied in the alchemy of my golden light that always beams upon you. What heals your mind, body and soul has been ordered for you and holds within it the best prescription on the planet – love, love, and more love. What once was, is no longer. Your wholeness has never been in question by God and will continue to be made so. We love you through eternity and beyond. May the light of you know this and feel our infinite blessings upon your soul and your life right now. And so it is."

Notes, inspired writing or other brainstorming ideas...

Day 345 – Archangel Metatron

"Stored anger in someone's body tends to lend itself to that person taking that negative energy out on others when they least expect it. If you should find yourself at the forefront of someone's repressed anger releasing, know that their troubles happened a long time ago and usually have nothing to do with you. Asking Archangel Michael to shield you with his light and sword from this usually initiates a positive charge in the room that almost immediately dissipates the negative charge being unleashed. What troubles someone else close to you does not need to penetrate your fibers. Use verbiage that supports and redirects the person to unleash elsewhere, but not on you. Your light shielding from Archangel Michael will become stronger as you set into motion this redirection pattern. Let your thoughts then go to what brings you peace, joy and ease of being. Your strength and stamina will continue to build as you do this."

Notes, inspired writing or other brainstorming ideas...

Day 346 — Archangel Ariel

"Dreaming into focus what you would most prefer to happen in your life assists us with bringing magical circumstances about for you. Ask us to assist you with more clarity if you are lacking focus in this area. When you dream and revise, dream and revise, dream and clarify, you magnify your mission by Divine Design. The clarity of your visions, no matter how many times you need to revise and design, delivers unto you the ultimate in magical manifestations the earth has yet to see. Your delivery system happens when you surrender that clarified vision for the benefit of the good of all. Be bold because the manifestation that will be delivered unto you will be even better than expected by calling in new form energy, aligned to Divine Will for the good of the entire earth. And so it is."

Notes, inspired writing or other brainstorming ideas...

Day 347 – Archangel Raphael

"Super-foods recharge your body and are a most excellent resource to nourish it with revitalizing nutrients and minerals. Bringing your body back into an equilibrium state of being that is well balanced and can sustain the stresses of everyday modern living often takes adding more whole, healthy foods and super-foods into your diet. Mother nature produces rich antioxidants that spring forth from the earth in abundance for you to enjoy. Loving yourself with foods that energize you instead of depleting you connect you to Divine Wisdom that plants and herbs contain. Adding richer, mineral dense foods into your diet also assist your brain wave patterns to hear your Guides and Angels more clearly because of the higher vibration frequencies that revitalizing foods and herbs hold for you. Food should be pleasurable. We love to see you experimenting with delectable recipes for all the nourishing rich foods your heart desires. Healing frequencies are also sent from the Angels into healthy food sources because foods born from Mother Earth can hold these healing vibrations much more resiliently. Call us in to bless the foods you prepare and we most certainly will in a heartbeat."

Notes, inspired writing or other brainstorming ideas...

Day 348 — Archangel Metatron

"Money is a resource of energy that flows in sync with your desires. What if that flow is stopped up in your life? The old form energy has and will continue to dissolve on earth. If one is trying to "get" money from old form ways of how money used to move through structured, rigid forms they may feel exhausted and tired a lot. Where does money come from through the new form you might ask? Money flows in a plethora of ways with the new light grids of God, from the Divine placed in and through Mother Earth and humanity. New form money flow comes from being aligned to one's Soul's Purpose, Life Purpose, and Divine Mission. Those that are out of the flow of their Soul's Calling will have a harder time bringing money in through endeavors that may have worked excellently in years past. What brings money flow now is aligning to God's Will, Your Soul's Purpose for your life. Being in sync with Mother Earth's rhythms will also open up the abundance flow for you. You'll receive a plethora of new ideas daily as you spend time with her. She is one of the greatest openers of the flow of money there is. If you ask her how you may serve and help humanity and her, she will show you the most Divine ways of helping the masses and receiving sustainable income through the abundance activating light grids that are on the planet now. Hopping into these magnetic abundant light energy lines that have been placed upon the planet by God, all the Archangels and Ascended Masters and asking how you may serve the good of all will usher an unimaginable flow of prosperity for the rest of your life. We encourage you to do this and feel the magic of all the blessings bestowed upon you."

Day 349 — Archangel Gabriel

"Your creative energy has a direct correlation to the foods you eat and nutrition intake. We love it when we see you eating high vibration foods that are rich in enzymes and minerals. When you are regularly consuming foods grown from Mother Earth's bounty of abundance, we are able to bring you ideas from the Divine Destiny Blueprint your soul has created for your life. What will work better; new ideas for sustained prosperity, light coded blueprints that will benefit the earth and all of her children. The light codes contained in freshly grown organic super foods, fruits and vegetables contain within them God Code Light. In this God Code Light is the leading edge of wisdom, encoded into every fiber of the organic produce. This heightens if you ask us to bless your produce before you eat it. We are able to deliver your Soul's Blueprints that is at the leading edge of consciousness and when ingested skyrockets your life into breakthroughs that take you from old consciousness thoughts and puts you at the center of the leading edge discoveries being made on earth at this time."

Notes, inspired writing or other brainstorming ideas...

Day 350 – Archangel Metatron

"This is an unprecedented time on earth, like no other. Claim your Divine Life Purpose and declare that the rest of it be revealed to you. Ask us to remove any of the doubt, obstacles or heaviness that may get in the way of you living your life within the new blueprints of earth that we have and continue to overlay onto the earth for all of humanity to hop into. When you enter into the Kingdom, what does this mean? Where is the Kingdom of heaven for you? The Kingdom of the Almighty is within you. However, in order to be "ascended" one must let go of the old form energy in order to enter into the light of the Kingdom we are bringing to the earth at this time, for all to be able to ascend to higher levels of God's wisdom as they are ready to do so. What brings your heart the most peace is living your life through this holy flow of God's light we are sending to earth in a never ending supply. There is enough for everyone. Allow the ride of the holy flow to take you to unprecedented heights. The lows will be superseded with the light of the Almighty. Yes, the transformation may be swift and you may be asked to let go of old habits that are not raising you up higher. In allowing the ascension of your life to continue, you are one of the great ones that will be remembered for your unyielding service in the most earth changing adventure ever."

Notes, inspired writing or other brainstorming ideas...

Day 351 – Archangel Michael

"Where can you serve, help, uplift and brighten someone's day? There are multitudes of deliverables at your table in bountiful glory. Ask us to bless your heart gift and deliver one to a friend this week or today. A gift from your heart goes a long way to another who may be feeling so low they can't get their head above water. The more that you give what you are inspired to share from your sacred heart space of love, the more Wisdom, Love, Tenderness and Divine Treasures you receive in return. Be willing to let it all hang out sometimes. It is through your authentic self being seen that you shall inherit earth's bounty for you. When your words, deeds and actions line up, Mother Earth replenishes your Divine Treasures again and again."

Notes, inspired writing or other brainstorming ideas...

Day 352 – Archangel Metatron

"Sometimes the ego wants to please others for the sake of receiving approval for a fleeting moment. What helps you stand in your humble power of love? Speaking specific words you are receiving as you are lined up to your true Divine power source. What holds you back sometimes is being afraid of upsetting others with your authentic words. There is a difference of being nice for the sake of stroking another's ego and firmly speaking what you are being led to speak because it is time to stand in who you really are completely. If it shall ruffle others feathers from humbly speaking your truth with love, call upon us to be there to show the other(s) Divine Wisdom so their lives may improve for the better. It is not your job to improve the lives of others, only to nurture what's true for you and shine like a summer sunrise allowing the dawn of a new day to rise again and again reflecting divinity herself through and through."

Notes, inspired writing or other brainstorming ideas...

Day 353 – Archangel Haniel

"Healing begins with understanding that to be in human form means embracing your imperfect self as much as possible. You were never asked to come to earth in order to "get perfect". Self-realization does not mean perfection. We want your self-realization to be fun, expansive and freeing. Not constricting yourself into fitting into society's latest fads or standards. Healing happens by a process of elimination. Eliminate all the things you force yourself to do that you no longer want to do. At the very least ask us for help with more soul-freeing solutions for all areas of your life you feel restricted in. Excavating what ultimately brings you joy, generates soul-level healing for you most naturally."

Notes, inspired writing or other brainstorming ideas...

Day 354 – Archangel Gabriel

"How much love you give is a direct reflection of the love that's inside waiting to burst forth like a spring flower in full bloom. To nourish this love flower it's important to water it daily with light from the Source. When you take time to be with the Creator to refill your inner well spring, you align with the never ending, always refilling streams of love. To rush yourself or hurry things into being is likened to pulling the flower out of the ground before there is even a bud. Savor and cherish the moments with the Divine like the most expensive wine or chocolate you've ever tasted. In those precious moments, what will be your creations are fed with soul love."

Notes, inspired writing or other brainstorming ideas...

Day 355 – Archangel Ariel

"We see that what used to drag you down is causing less and less turmoil within you. You have been willing to brave many storms and find the jewels in them. You are a diamond in the rough. We'd like you to remember that about yourself. Trust that if upheaval should occur again you now have the tools to remember how to respond from that peaceful wise place you are so good at entering into. Continue asking "What will work even better for me that will also raise the consciousness of mankind?" As sure as you ask the question, the answer has already arrived. You are a vibrant soul upon the earth. Never allow your light to be dimmed by anyone who seems to know more than you. For what sets you free the most is turning your light dial up to full blast sometimes. There you'll find the seeds of your greatness waiting for pure sunlight and salt-mineralized water to nourish your true soul's essence."

Notes, inspired writing or other brainstorming ideas. . .

Day 356 — Archangel Raphael

"Eating sun ripened berries such as Goji berries helps heal your vital resources from within. Resting more with your feet in the earth and your creative writing journal at hand draws in from the ethers Angel Restoration Energy from us. When you are doubting your abilities and doubting self, call us in and write it out. Ask us questions on paper and listen for our response. You'll get a more crystal clear sense of how we view you, which is always through the eyes of Divine Love and seeing your greatness. Building up your inner reservoirs of healing and internal sustaining energy helps you see yourself this way too. It nurtures the body and brings vitality to your body, mind, connection in the most magical of ways. The essence of who you really are never leaves you. What delivers love to you, serves it to all in rainbows of delightful ways."

Notes, inspired writing or other brainstorming ideas . . .

Day 357 — Archangel Michael

"What may assist you in feeling more balanced is short intentional periods rest 2 - 3 times per day. 10 minute segments of listening to peaceful music while gazing at nature or the sky with your feet grounded upon the grass or dirt will reset your emotional, physical and mental state of well-being. By scheduling in these break segments as part of your daily activities your body will be able to maintain better homeostasis. What you'll find is that what needs to get done as a priority item will have a smoother flow of getting done when miniature renewal segments are deliberately taken. Suddenly you may get inspired ideas of how to schedule in the most pressing items differently so that when your energy is lagging, your body will know a renewal of energy is coming up. Call us in if you'd like when you grab these resetting periods. We will send frequencies of renewal that will rejuvenate you in double time – 10 minutes will feel like 20 minutes with how rested and ready to go you'll feel. We are always available for you for these types of requests. Nothing is too small to ask of us. We are here to energize you and light the path before you."

Notes, inspired writing or other brainstorming ideas...

Day 358 – Archangel Raphael

"The epidemic of cancer is far-reaching right now. When someone you know has cancer it is best to suggest things, but never to force anything upon that person that you think they "should" be doing. Cancer is a great teacher, that's why many are allowing themselves to get it. From the overview of their soul's perspective, it is showing them to trust their natural internal instincts again and to understand what wants to be transformed in the way their life was running to be melted down like glistening snow turning into running water. To assist those with cancer, be kind in your mind with them. The pattern with those who have cancers tends to be very harsh on themselves in their minds already about what "should" be happening that is not. Praying for their healing does indeed assist more healing light to reach them. Usually those with cancer are incredibly strong souls. Ask that they be shown what healing modalities would be best for them to choose. The protocol of what would work best may vary from person to person. There is not one "right" way to their alignment. What works for one, may not work for the next. Sing praises for their healing, as if it were complete. You may simply say, "May Thy will be done, on earth as it is in heaven," for them. Your good thoughts towards them really helps to uplift their spirits. One day they may not even realize that they suddenly feel better and what brought in more healing light were that two of their closest and dearest friends said prayers for them that day and it gave us Angels permission to usher in Divine Healing Light. Your prayers and open-minded loving thoughts make a tremendous amount of difference. The healing light that returns to you from every heartfelt, sincere prayer you send brings back quadruple in healing energy for you upon your life and your good health. What you sow you shall reap. Sow infinite prayers for others and the good of humanity and Divine Light returns to you infinite healing blessings."

Day 359 – Archangel Ariel

"Clarifying what helps you stand on your own two feet, while in the effortless flow of living your dreams is where your Divine Destiny meets effortless expansion. Your life design that is for the highest and best good of all of humanity has been designed by you with us and your soul. What causes you anxiety and to feel ungrounded pulls you further away from it. What brings your heart peace is where we beckon you forward, for therein love remains for you. None of the glamour and frills matter much in the end. What brings you love and peace forever will be knowing the hearts that you touched. Allow your Divine Destiny Design to be birthed from the most sacred part of yourself. Let troubles of the mind be replaced by love for all that is good, all that is soul nourishing. What heals your soul sends frequency waves of cosmic love that wrap around the planet so all may benefit. Your love is never ending, always beginning anew. The expansion of you knows that all is possible as it is brought into this world from peaceful inward journeys of the heart."

Notes, inspired writing or other brainstorming ideas...

Day 360 – Archangel Michael

"When you want something but don't feel you can have it yet, know that it is already on its way if it is aligned to the highest and best good of all involved. When you feel you have lost out on something check your inner resources and tune in to see what you feel you have neglected to give yourself that would energize your body, mind and soul. Where you feel you are lacking on the outside can be found as a voided space from within. Close your eyes for a moment and feel into the area on the inside of you as you breathe in... feeling where the not enoughness is. Ask this part of yourself what does enough love look like? Which ones would bring you long lasting, ever-giving pure joy? Once these are highlighted for you, you'll realize you have never been lacking in the first place. All the answers can be found from within and your sustained joy comes from feeling into what is in the flow of your Divine Joy versus what falls flat or could potentially become a sore thumb. We assist you today with seeing what lifts you to your ultimate joy levels here on earth."

Notes, inspired writing or other brainstorming ideas . . .

Day 361 — Archangel Gabriel

"The love of you knows there's nothing ever lost. What seems like a loss is only a transformation to something way more fulfilling for your heart, body, mind and soul. We are smiling for you today. Cheers to a Divine Arena with showers of golden light sprinkles of love. This is a new beginning for you our friend. Your time has arrived and is blessed immaculately by us and the Divine. We want you to know you are worthy of receiving this. What has been created through love will be blessed with infinite amounts of love gifts of the heart for you. Your dues are paid. Now it is time for you to celebrate through the peace of knowing that all that is good is on its way to you."

Notes, inspired writing or other brainstorming ideas . . .

Day 362 — Archangel Raphael

"What restores your energy and vitality elevates the consciousness of the entire planet and species. You in-taking more living foods for more sustainable energy creates a vibration in all of your cells so that inside your light body which communicates with others who are speaking with you, they pick up on the fact that your body, mind and soul is alive with some kind of magical energy. The secrets of Mother Earth are contained within your living cell's walls. Suddenly after eating foods that are more whole and alive you'll often receive ideas of new ways of living or how to improve your life or the lives of others in some way. The flow of ancient wisdom is inside foods that grow from the earth, there is no other way around it. Eat for replenishment through richly colored foods and herbs and you'll have solutions to any problems or ailments within weeks, often days. What would you automatically want to feed a growing toddler? Your body's longevity is calling out for the same."

Notes, inspired writing or other brainstorming ideas...

Day 363 — Archangel Michael

"The tenderness of your love for others depends upon how sweet your love is for self. Are you selfish if you love yourself wholeheartedly? What develops as an obsession in others is not feeling completely loved and nurtured from within to begin with. Seeking outside fulfillment to fill inside cravings is like putting a Band-Aid on an infected wound without cleaning it and giving it healing salves first. The fester of the cravings just get more demanding. To heal the wound, cosmic love is needed. The love that goes beyond this world is what each soul is really seeking. Allow God's love to ride in like a prism light beam from the ethers. Divinity wants you to call God's light in more. Light entering the earth from the ethers begets more light. The Cosmic Dance of your soul is eternal. To remember your eternal self is to dance in the love of the Cosmic Flame."

Notes, inspired writing or other brainstorming ideas...

Day 364 – Archangel Metatron

"Many are feeling stirred up right now on earth and very unsettled. What used to work for some to calm themselves down is not as effective. This is because the rhythms of Mother Earth are shifting into the higher dimensions of light and this is causing a lot of releasing of the old ways. Those that live in larger cities with less open nature to go into are having the roughest time. It is key to remember, where there is great turmoil has the most potential for future advancement and connection to source light. The old energies upon the earth need to transform so a new lighter order of what would work better in your life and in the lives of all of humanity can come in. All of us Archangels are assisting this most intense change of earth's ways right now. What creates peace and deep harmony with you and each person on earth is what is important. When you are at peace, a new order for how your life could work better can be found from within more readily. What once was, is no longer. Call us in to help this change you are going through be more gentle and lighter, for it can be. You are a pillar of light for the entire planet. The more you are drawn to call upon us the easier this transition will be for you. What once gripped you with panic and fear will leave you unscathed the more you ask for our assistance. There is no more profound time to ask for more assistance, than there is right now. Your golden key is in the asking."

Notes, inspired writing or other brainstorming ideas...

Day 365 – Archangel Gabriel

"Seeking too much advice outside of yourself can sometimes lead you further astray than learning how to tune in and "know" which way to go would be best for you. We always advise seeking out help in the form of more knowledgeable people, but if in doing so that leaves you feeling less joyful, like something in your gut wants you to go a different way than the experts' advice you may be pleasantly surprised when miracles happen. As you are getting really good at tuning into what feels like love to you and what feels incredibly uplifting for you with an added feeling of freedom, this is how you know the direction you are going is meant for you. We can also help clarify for you what would be absolutely beneficial for you and what advice may be leading you further off your path and Divine Flow. Others will always put in their two cents worth of advice. The joy that you feel after you make the decision is your compass towards your Divinely Designed Destiny Path. Ask us for even more viable solutions and rest assured they are already on their way."

Notes, inspired writing or other brainstorming ideas...

Day 366 — Archangel Michael

"On those days you feel things just can't get any worse, therein resides a window of hope for you from us. The length of your travesty has no precedence. Allow your thoughts to go soft on those days and allow us to show you an alternate way of looking at what troubles you. Just as there is wind and solar power now, your light body is also being upgraded so that it functions ideally with the higher light grids that have been placed upon the planet for her easier transition into a higher state of being as well. When you are in the holy flow of allowing yourself to be guided to other solutions for the long standing problems that are at hand, the resistance and blocks in your body systems can be loosened and transformed by us more easily. Going to an effortless flow, instead of fighting the current brings you to the center point of Golden Divine Light where the muck and the mire do not exist. As you enter into Divine Grace a plethora of solutions suddenly become visible all around you. Divine Grace is your natural state of being. This is what you are being lifted up into so that the entanglements of yesteryear's troubles vanish in the presence of Divine Grace. Events, circumstances, helpful people and new pliable options become fully tangible when a state of Divine Grace circumvents the chaos."

Notes, inspired writing or other brainstorming ideas...

Day 367 — Archangel Raphael

"Taking care of everyone else first only leads to depletion within the body, mind and spirit. I am working diligently with you, teaming up with you so that you fill up your own cup first thing in the morning. Drinking water as soon as you awake, breathing in some fresh air and spending some time in quiet prayer or contemplation brings Divine Flow to the start of your day. When you hop right into tasks in the morning and give away that vital morning yin energy to others before yourself this sets up your body's energy flow to deplete itself quite early in the day. When you take the time to nourish yourself with good healing foods and herbal tonics your energetic field can set up a robust protection for you so any stresses that should occur during the day bounce off of your auric field instead of fragmenting it and depleting it. What brings you peace, brings the world more peace and oh, how the world needs more peace from everyone right now. May you be well, our friend and know how much you are looked after. The love we have for you is unyielding and never ending."

Notes, inspired writing or other brainstorming ideas...

Day 368 — Archangel Gabriel

"Your perspective is important and DOES matter. You have arrived at the exact place in time where all you desire can be born through you. The obstacles and old shackles have been removed. What do you most want? I, Gabriel will help you with this. Write this down and all of the Archangels, including myself will be rolling up our sleeves to assist you with this in every way possible. Be at peace and visualize this coming to be."

Notes, inspired writing or other brainstorming ideas...

Recommended Resources for Empaths...

9 **FREE** Archangel Michael Prayers of Protection PDF

Anxiety Relief Archangel Michael **FREE** Meditation

Hear Your Angels & Guides Better **FREE** Video

Archangel Michael House Clearing & Blessing Audio Download

Archangel Crystal Light Healing Sessions

Archangel Crystal Light Unit for Healers and Home Use

Chakra Cleansing & Blessings with the Archangels LIVE EVENTS

You can find all of the resources mentioned above at:

ArchangelsBless.com

One Last Thing...

If you enjoyed this journal or found it useful, I'd be very grateful if you'd post a short review on Amazon. Your support does make a difference, and I read all the reviews personally so I can get your feedback and make this journal even better.

Thanks again for leaving a quick review!

Made in the USA
Middletown, DE
21 September 2020